7 SECRETS EVERY COMMODITY TRADER NEEDS TO KNOW

A GUIDE TO BECOMING A MASTER TRADER

JAMES MOUND

Traders Press, Inc.®
PO Box 6206
Greenville, SC 29606

Serving Traders since 1975

Editing and Cover Design
Teresa Darty Alligood
Editor and Graphic Designer
Traders Press, Inc.®

Traders Press, Inc.®
PO Box 6206
Greenville, SC 29606

Serving Traders since 1975

http://www.traderspress.com

Dedication

*To those who have inspired me
to find happiness and success in what life
has to offer Thank You.*

TABLE OF CONTENTS

Publisher's Foreword

Trading futures profitably is not an easy undertaking. I can attest to this from decades of personal experience. An early interest in trading stocks, beginning at age twelve, evolved into a lifelong interest in futures trading, beginning with my senior year in college in 1967. The first foray into the futures trading jungle resulted in the loss of my entire trading capital, $8,000, which had been earned at 80 cents per hour working at my father's lumber yard, and in my college library after a raise to $1.00 per hour. Not to be discouraged easily, I scrimped and saved until I had another grubstake of $5,000. This "second start" resulted, again, in a total loss of my trading capital. Patiently, I went through this process twice more in the ensuing years until, years later, I finally "turned the corner" and began trading profitably. Ironically, this was after having achieved financial stability and security, after I could "afford to lose".

When I first began trading, one could count on the fingers of one hand the books in print which gave worthwhile advice on trading in futures. The principles that James Mound teaches so well in this book would have done me much good when I began trading futures, and might well have made a significant difference in my learning curve. New traders today will find sound advice in here, and should take the lessons that are offered to heart. They may well save you from the experience that I had myself, and put you on the road to profitable trading much sooner than I myself found the path.

Edward Dobson

Edward D. Dobson, President
Traders Press, Inc.®
Greenville, South Carolina

December 26, 2002

Introduction

The stock market has always intrigued me. The dynamics of finding sound companies prime for growth and profiting from their successes has an overwhelming attraction to most investors. Commodities, a shrinking investment realm by comparison, has always given the appearance of an all or nothing, rags to riches, dreamland. The truth is, however, commodities is enriched by concrete concepts and leveraged opportunities while the stock market holds the dreams of the derivative ownership in a company made up of more unknowns to the average investor than one would care to acknowledge.

My interest in commodities came about when I was introduced to leverage.Imagine being able to find a profitable strategy and then using the concept of leveraging your capital to create an exponential growth of profits. This is not merely a fantasy, but a reality found when properly investing in these markets. This book is designed to show you how to accomplish this ultimate goal by becoming a complete trader.

What is a complete trader? A complete trader is one who maximizes their utilization of all of the tools and information available to them within a given market. This means combining the knowledge of technical tools and charting, gaining scope and perspective on the historical and present fundamentals of a market, and using proper trade designs to accomplish a risk managed and profit maximizing approach. Thus, using the tools and information available to minimize mistakes, control losses and maximize trade design to accomplish consistency in profitability. Every one of the secrets you are about to uncover in this book are about making you a complete trader. Anyone can make some simple technical forecasts, gain knowledge of the fundamental history of a market, and use futures or options to trade a market. But how many traders can make the analysis and decisions necessary to be a consistently profitable trader?

While exact figures vary depending on who you ask, they say 90% of commodities traders lose money. Only one out of ten will make money in this business; how is that possible? The majority of traders lose money because of lack of knowledge and understanding. Successful traders have knowledge, patience, lack of emotion, and perspective to make controlled investment decisions. As you read "7 Secrets" you will begin to grasp what it takes to be a profitable trader. There are no free lunches, can't miss trades, or windfall opportunities. Discipline, research, experience and patience make successful traders. You can be one of these traders if you take the steps outlined in this book to bring your investment skills to the next level; the level of a master trader.

AUTHOR'S NOTE: You will make the most out of the experience of reading "7 Secrets" if you have an understanding of the following prior to reading this book:

* How supply and demand affect market price
* The dynamics of simple technical tools like stochastics, moving averages, trend line support and resistance, etc.
* The concept of leverage as applied to commodity trading
* Basic knowledge and definitions of options and simple option strategies
* The definitions and usage of order placement techniques (stops, spreads, etc.)

SECRET #1
MASTERING THE MARKETS YOU
TRADE...FUNDAMENTALS

Not spending the time to understand the market you are trading is a common mistake among traders. To master a market one must fully grasp the market's historical, present and future fundamental, technical (secret #2), and volume characteristics (secret #3). Once you master these key aspects of a market you will gain the perspective necessary to control risk, maximize profit and determine trading opportunities in almost any market condition.

Market fundamentals are an ever-present determinate of price and volatility in every market. Understanding what those fundamentals are, for the market you are trading, is the first step. To answer the question of what fundamentals truly control a market, one must discover what controls the supply and demand element of that particular market.

For instance, grains have one of the simplest to understand but hardest to forecast fundamental structures. The supply fundamentals built into the grain market are plantings, production, inventories, and weather. Demand is made up of inventories, usage and substitutive commodities (i.e. wheat and corn are substitutive commodities because either can be used as cattle feed depending on which is the best price). Every commodity has different elements that make up the supply and demand structure. Once a trader grasps these fundamental aspects of the commodity they are trading, you can begin to utilize information to predict potential changes/fluctuations in the market. All assumed fundamentals are built into the market, while speculation occurs when certain fundamentals are in question.

A common mistake of traders is that they analyze the present and future fundamentals of a market while only using technicals to ascertain historical price movement. If traders would simply combine technical history with fundamental history, price movements would be much more predictable. For example, the OJ market typically has price spikes during the months of October and January due to critical USDA reports on the plantings, inventories, harvest and frost conditions that comes out early in both months. However, understanding the fundamentals of the market during years where an October or January spike was seen, versus years when it was not seen, would better allow traders to predict whether present fundamental conditions exist to suggest a similar spike (#1.1)

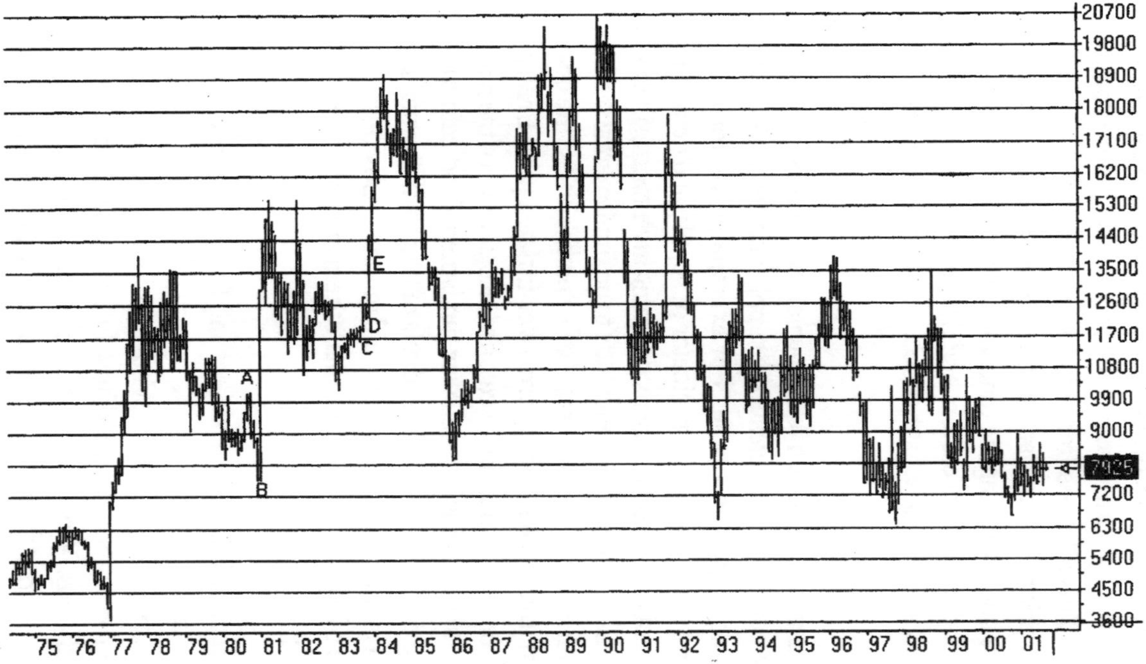

Chart 1-1
Monthly OJ

In the October 1980 USDA report a market let down, on solid crop numbers and little expectation for crop damage (A), was followed by a massive reversal led on by confirmation from the January 1981 report of crop damage and ongoing crop problems (B). In 1983, a mild yet positive October report sparked a surge in prices (C) that was only complemented by weather conditions (D) and a January report confirming serious crop problems. A quick study of these two examples illustrates the obvious fundamental observation that the October report is a potential precursor to future price movements, yet it is merely a forecasting tool that can only be confirmed by real events in the future. The January study shows more realistic and quantifiable results and therefore has stronger and more founded price movements. Using this knowledge of the historic fundamental impacts of these reports on prices, helps the investor more accurately gauge current fundamental and technical market indicators.

It is highly recommended that a trader spends the time to research the full fundamental history of a market prior to trading it. Always look at the fundamental history of a market before doing anything else. This allows a trader to have a complete scope of market activity prior to looking at the other elements of researching a market. After understanding the fundamental history of a market it becomes easier to analyze current and future fundamentals because you can compare it to what has occurred in that market over its history.

Keep in mind that certain fundamentals become less or more relevant as the conditions that create the supply and demand structure of a market change over time. For example, inventories in silver have long been a powerful indicator of supply and demand. However in recent years, despite heavily declining inventories, silver's price has generally trended down with little to no fundamental influences. This can be attributed to a number of possibilities: the unknown foreign inventories, a long term over-inflated price finally coming down, or little interest in inventories. Regardless of the reason, it is vital to avoid including irrelevant fundamental indicators in making trading decisions. As a general rule of thumb, if the market ignores it and it is widely known, you should ignore it. Obviously, if you are aware of a potential change that others are not, then this would not apply.

Market price is based on present and future fundamentals, with historical fundamentals being the framework within what picture the current ones are analyzed. What is built into the market is what the current conditions are, and how future fundamentals will alter these conditions. What traders must ask themselves is what is it that is creating market fluctuations? Within this answer is the key to grasping potential future price movement and thereby creating trading opportunities. Present and future fundamentals cause price fluctuations when supply and/or demand is in question. Reports, forecasts, weather, substitutive commodities, technology, politics and government, and production changes can all affect supply and/or demand and therefore create price fluctuation.

Reports and forecasts generate expectations or actual figures of supply and demand in a market. Build up to reports cause speculation and rumors within a market. This can actually cause more volatility and price fluctuation than the actual report, especially when very little is known ahead of the report. Because you already have gained the historical perspective of any given report, you can begin to grasp the market movement before and after the report you are analyzing. You must ask yourself a number of qualifying questions to give yourself perspective and direction prior to a report. What is the current supply and demand structure of the market? How will this report affect that structure? What is assumed about the report? Should these facts be assumed by the market participants? What is not assumed? How will these unknown factors affect supply and/or demand, and therefore price? What is the time frame that this report will have an effect on supply and/or demand? How do the potential fundamental changes from the report compare to historical effects of the same or similar reports? Answering these questions will go a long way to telling an investor what to expect out of the market during the days up to and days following the release of the report.

Reports are all about volatility prior to and immediately following the release, and trending from the report once it is 'digested' by the market participants. An example of such activity can be found in all markets. Cattle, for instance, has monthly slaughter reports that tend to create volatility up to the report, a spike reaction and trending thereafter (#1.2).

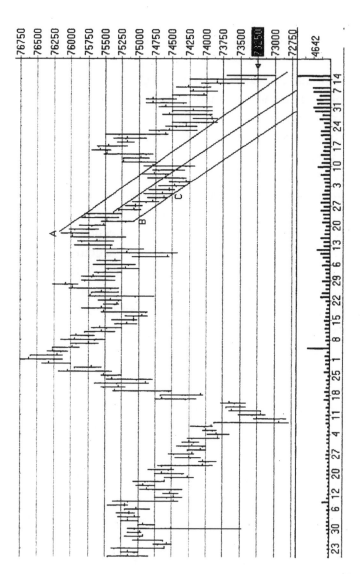

Chart 1-2
Daily Dec. '01 Live Cattle

In this example, solid buying was seen ahead of the report (A), followed by a swift selloff just days prior to the report (profit taking and the other side of the seesaw speculating that goes on before a report) (A to B). On the day of the report the market reacts with a full on selloff, thereby confirming the reversal (B). This trend continues as the market adjusts to the change in fundamentals and appropriate price correction (C).

Weather has a profound affect on the supply and demand structure of all harvested commodities. Activity due to weather fundamentals has been the cause of some of the largest price moves in the history of commodities. Weather, however, is a tricky thing. It is difficult to predict timing, location and affect of weather elements in a market, as well as how the market participants will perceive it. While difficult to predict weather elements within a given market, the tried and true method of seasonal and cyclical forecasting tends to work best. Using almanacs to determine statistical probability of weather affects on a market is the first step. What is the highest number of consecutive years a market has been unaffected by weather? What is the lowest? What is the average? What is the timing within a year that has the greatest statistical probability to affect the market? Where is the current price within that period, and how does that compare to historical pricing at that time? A simple statistical program can determine probability of weather, although most markets have that type of information publicly available. Knowing the answers to these questions allows a trader to maximize trade design and timing and prevent vulnerability to negative exposure of such moves.

The market sometimes gets ahead of itself when it comes to weather fundamentals, thereby creating enormous volatility and swift reversals when the market is wrong. Coffee is a perfect example. With a powerful element of frost during growing season, the market has been known to move as much as 50% in just days if weather indicates the potential for damage to the crop. We all know forecasts can be wrong, but traders that are short a market are quick to exit as fear enters the market. Speculators want to be ahead of the move, and before the weather is known the market has already factored most of the potential damage into the price of the commodity. The coffee market is by no means the exception. (#1.3)

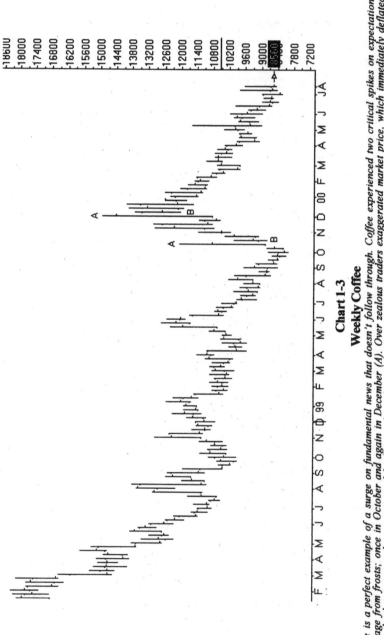

Chart 1-3

Weekly Coffee

Here is a perfect example of a surge on fundamental news that doesn't follow through. Coffee experienced two critical spikes on expectations of crop damage from frosts; once in October and again in December (A). Over zealous traders exaggerated market price, which immediately deflated (B) and came back to a normal expectation of fundamental conditions and correlating market price.

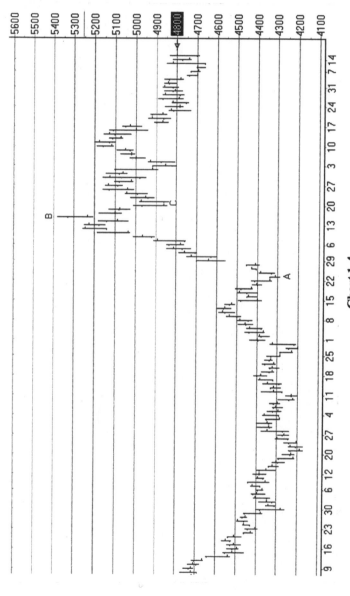

Chart 1-4
Daily Nov. '01 Soybeans

On this price chart, the market has an ahead of the news rally, hoping to surge on potential weather fundamentals (A), surging over 25% in 16 trading days (A to B). Once it appears there is little chance for a follow-through on the weather (B), the market plummets almost 10% in just 4 days (C), thus illustrating the overwhelming power the market has to correct itself when expectations over-exaggerate market prices.

Understanding substitutive commodities is an important element to gauging many markets. The idea behind substitutive commodities is that when the price of one commodity goes out of whack as compared to another that can be used in its place, the market's tendency is to have a 'sympathy' move of the secondary commodity. This is done because supply and demand tends to fluctuate under these circumstances. For example, wheat is used as cattle feed, but so is corn. Wheat prices rally because of a large order from China to import wheat. What then, happens to corn? Corn, although nothing fundamental appears to have occurred, will tend to rally behind wheat prices as wheat buyers turn to corn's cheaper price to use for feed in place of the more expensive wheat. So, while nothing fundamental has occurred in the corn market, demand has increased because of its use as a substitutive commodity. A trader must be aware of elements outside of the market they are trading that affect them in order to be a master trader.

Technological advances, while not always present in a commodity, can sometimes affect price. For example, a recent outbreak of fruit flies in Florida oranges should have sent prices through the roof. However, due to the recent advances, chemicals to protect crops and reduce outbreaks created a relative non-reaction in the market. A current technological advance in the corn market is genetically manufactured or biogenetic corn, which allows for a potential flooding of supply from industry and not farmers. This could put farmers out of business by over supplying the market, and potentially drag down other grains as a substitutive commodity. Regardless, technology is an element of market fundamentals to be aware of, and is a reason to stay on top of current news and events in order to protect yourself.

Political and governmental influences on markets are perhaps the most critical, constant and profound fundamental elements present in commodities today. We see these influences in almost every market, from OPEC's control and corruption over the energy markets, to the FOMC's power to essentially dictate US and world-wide interest rate policy. I relate it to swimming in rapids. If you have ever swam a rapid you know that while it appears that you should have control you have absolutely none. Similarly, the trader constantly swims in the government's river of power, merrily picking fish until a big rapid comes crashing down and the reality hits that they control everything; they're just good at hiding in the water. There are two divisions of influence these powers have on the market: scheduled and unscheduled. The difference is everything.

FOMC (Federal Open Market Committee) meetings, held 8 times annually, have a tremendous impact on interest rates and the overall pricing of the bond market. This is a scheduled influence on the market, and such government intervention into market activity is normally welcomed volatility. These reports dictate, more than any other influence, the future of these markets. Typically, market activity up to the report is volatile and choppy as market participants fight for positioning and the stronger opinion moves the market to one side or the other. It also sets option premiums at high levels and establishes a predictable level of market volatility going into the report. Such scheduled meetings tend to get publicity and are widely known prior to the report. Moreover, the forecasts are also well publicized, and a major influence heading into the report. Because of these 'knowns', the probability of market surprise is reduced and historic volatility can be used to predict expected volatility with relative ease. Scheduled reports can be trend setters or trend followers (trend being the operative word). (#1.5)

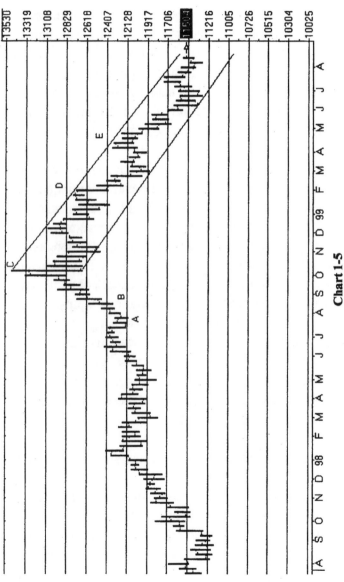

Chart 1-5

Weekly 30 yr. T-Bond

Market volatility increases in relation to speculative interest as FOMC reports near. The price speculation tends to follow the direction the market 'hopes' the Fed will go, rather than the trend of the interest policy the Fed is following. Point (A) illustrates the market pushing the price towards topside resistance, then the Fed follows through with the market's 'hope' and the breakout follows the overall trend of the market (B). When the next Fed meeting (C) reverses the policy trend, the market reacts with a massive price reversal followed by trending which is supported by future Fed announcements that complement the declining trend (D&E).

While the FOMC meeting is a known and somewhat predictable event, government influences can be most profound when an unscheduled event takes the market off guard. For the most part, these unscheduled events have little volatility up to the time of the event. This depends on how much information is known, but assuming little to no information is present prior to the event the market must then react instantly. This causes a whirlwind affect on the market. Generally an overreaction followed by a swift correction is a common reaction to such unexpected events.

So how does a trader gauge potential government involvement in a market? This is one of the hardest events for the individual speculator to gauge. Typically, experienced market participants will look for hints from government reports and announcements. For instance, the Federal Reserve includes comments of interest rate policy going forward with their FOMC reports. OPEC officials leak news of potential policy moves to get feedback of public and political reactions. Foreign powerhouse governments put pressure on economically challenged countries to make changes (yen intervention, Brazilian inflation woes, etc.). The warning signs are everywhere, but predictability is generally absent. This is all about market awareness; knowing the influences on market conditions and keeping a strong level of monitoring of these influences as a constant backdrop to a trader's research.

Cocoa presents a decent story to illustrate the true power of political influence, and how awareness can help a trader to master the market they trade. The Ivory Coast, the largest producer of cocoa in the world, recently experienced the affects of political and governmental influence on its core market. For as far back as anyone can remember, the Ivory Coast paid their farmers a standard wage for their cocoa crops. With cocoa prices above 1600, cocoa farmers began to revolt as enormous profits were being taken by the government and not the farmers. The government finally agreed to pay the farmers on a percentage of profits basis. Cocoa prices swiftly dropped to less than half of its 1600 price in less than 12 months. With little to no profit left in cocoa prices, the farmers began to burn crops, assassinated numerous government officials and attempted a number of coups. This caused volatility in the price of cocoa, but no upward movement seemed to stick. The government overpowered the uprising. A master trader would have shorted the market spikes and made a fortune; just by having a scope of the market, and realizing the inability of these farmers to ultimately influence the government's actions. If you master the fundamentals, you are well on your way to mastering the markets you trade. (#1.6)

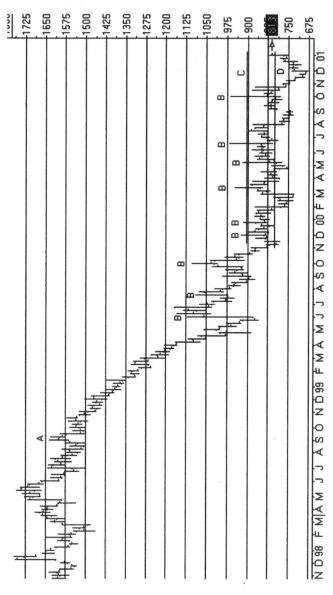

Chart 1-6

Weekly Cocoa

After the government's reaction to the farmers demand for being paid a percentage of profits, the market went from prices in the 1600 area (A) to a massive decline where prices wandered between 750 and 1000. Over this period, price spikes on news and rumors of civil strife and coups (B) were met with quick selloffs when nothing seem to materialize. Buying around 800 (D) and selling on spikes through 900 (C) provided numerous profit opportunities during this period of uncertainty for market participants. Those who understood the dynamics of the situation were able to monopolize the profits in this market.

Changes in production quite often can spark a change in speculative sentiment, and therefore cause dramatic price movements. One must look to identify patterns in production versus price in their particular market in order to master this aspect of fundamental change. Typically, but not always, production changes are based on price movements, as seen most recently with OPEC's attempts to control production in order to boost crude oil prices.

In February of 1999, with crude futures trading at $11 a barrel, OPEC made a historic move to force the world's largest oil producing nations to pull back production in order to create a more reasonable and profitable price range for energy markets. Within two years crude oil prices had tripled, based almost entirely on OPEC's efforts. This in many ways combines both a political influence and a production change. However, regardless of whom is causing the change in production, this example illustrates just how much of a long term and powerful of an effect a production change can have on a market. It also illustrates that production changes are typically a result of far reaching prices; a reaction to supply and demand versus price.

How does one go about predicting future production changes? You don't. When OPEC announced its retention plan the market was unprepared for its effectiveness. Interpreting this change in production is how one masters the market fundamentals. If crude's break even production costs are around $18 a gallon, and a range of $18 to $25 would be reasonable for profitable production, wouldn't it then be safe to assume that should this retention plan be successful that we would at least hit $18? Also, given a market's tendency to play both sides of a range before settling in the middle, wouldn't it be logical to see crude oil eventually test the upper limits of $25 a barrel or more? The trend took almost two years to top off, which is plenty of time to jump on a market when a massive production overhaul such as this takes place. Analyze the change and its impending affects on its market, and you will profit from the price change that follows.

Regardless of the cause of a fundamental shift in a market, the keys to mastering fundamentals and profiting from them are clear. First, you must identify and create awareness of the historical significance of the fundamentals that affect a market's supply and demand. Then attempt to identify the warning signs of future fundamental changes and their potential affect on price. Finally, take a step back to grasp the full nature of a market's supply and demand and the inner workings of a fundamental change's influence on the market. If you can do this, you have mastered the analysis of market fundamentals and are on the road to becoming an expert trader.

FREE BOOK AND TRADER'S CATALOG!!

Send us your name and address and we'll send you our 100-page *TRADER'S CATALOG* and your choice of one of the books listed below *FREE!*

NAME _____

ADDRESS _____

CITY _____ **ST** _____ **ZIP** _____

E-MAIL ADDRESS _____

If replying by phone, fax, or e-mail, refer to the code shown in the box to the right:

328996-2

FREE BOOK CHOICE: Please send me your catalog and the following free book: (circle your choice, limit 1)**Safe Sex on Wall Street **Understanding Fibonacci Numbers **Protecting Your Net Worth.

RETURN OR REPLY TO: Traders Press, Inc. PO Box 6206, Greenville, SC 29606 (800-927-8222; 864-298-0222; fax 864-298-0221; E-mail request to: catalog@traderspress.com.)

SECRET #2
HOW TO USE TECHNICAL INDICATORS...PROPERLY

Those who believe that historical price movement predicts future price movement are considered technical traders. These technical traders utilize dozens of technical tools to decipher what the price movement in the market is telling them about what will happen next. Technical trading is a mathematical science that takes many lifetimes to master, which is why we use indicators that have been created through the work of many mathematicians. In this chapter all aspects of technical trading will be reviewed; everything from system trading to which technical tools work and which do not.

Unfortunately, technical traders are just that; technical traders. They ignore the other elements used in trading decisions and market analysis. To be a complete trader (the goal of this book), one must compliment their analysis with the tools they use. A fundamentalist ignores technical indicators, and a technical analyst ignores fundamentals (and everyone ignores volume). When a technical trader makes an error in judgment it is inevitably due to one reason: history appears to not repeat itself. This is rarely the case, but it does appear to a technical trader this way. What is truly occurring is the failure of the trader to analyze other elements, ones that show the differences between the historical pattern and the current one. Technical trading is the science of using historical patterns to predict future results. The key to using this science is being able to identify those patterns. When technical traders fail in this respect it is because the chart has lied (or at least their perception of the chart). History never lies, but your eyes do. This is certainly a difficult, yet important, concept to grasp. Fundamentals are often ignored in technical analysis because it is theoretically built into the technical price history of a market. Yet it never fails that a technical pattern to a technical trader becomes the bible to a market, when a proper viewpoint is to combine the technical chart patterns with a fundamental structure that would *complement* that pattern. Then you may have a trade on your hands.

It is vital to utilize charts with a complete understanding of the fundamental elements that have created these historical technical moves. A trader can maximize their technical analysis by matching technical history with fundamental history. When a chart shows a pattern that is repeated within its history, but does not have the same fundamental structure or seasonal timing, the traders needs to breakdown these differences. Once the differences are know a trader can then have a true comparison and determine whether or not the differences would affect the matching pattern. Common technical tools utilize just the technical pattern without relying on historical significance. What if a chart pattern isn't relying on a correlating historical pattern? The trader should then look through the historical charting to determine if this pattern had existed in the past and then figure out whether the pattern had a tendency to follow through with the expected move. If not, the trader needs to verify that the historical indicator had different fundamental aspects to make a lack of a follow through explainable. Otherwise, the pattern must be questioned. Technical indicators are only valuable if they are verified through fundamental and technical history.

For every technical indicator you show me that says a market is going one way, I can show one that says the opposite. If this is true, then what value do these indicators really have? They have a tremendous value if you can decipher which indicators are relevant and which are not. This varies from market to market, and by tool and time frame. Every technical trading method has a market that gives it significance, timing that gives it accuracy, and historical relevance to create profitability. The real asset with technical trading is mastering the tools that accurately predict a given market at a given time. If you can do this then you can truly benefit from the right technical tools and identify the wrong ones that you should ignore. The secret to technical trading is understanding historical relevance, significance and time frame. This chapter will utilize some of the simplest of technical tools to show these points.

After running the gamut from the simplest of technical tools to some of the most complex and difficult approaches, one actually finds simpler is almost always better. Occam's razor, a scientific term and theory of problem solving, suggests that when in doubt the simplest explanation proves to be the best one. This tends to apply to the application of technical indicators. Why use a complex approach when a simple one explains the same price movement? Here are some examples of proper approaches to technical analysis using some simple technical tools (it assumed that you have relative mastery of these techniques prior to reading what follows).

Let's look at three simple technical tools to illustrate proper identification of historical relevance, significance and time frame. Stochastics, simple moving averages, and support and resistance points are common tools used to help traders determine entry and exit points, stops and timing. The following is intended to show the proper method of using technical tools to predict and analyze markets, thereby releasing the secret to successful technical trading.

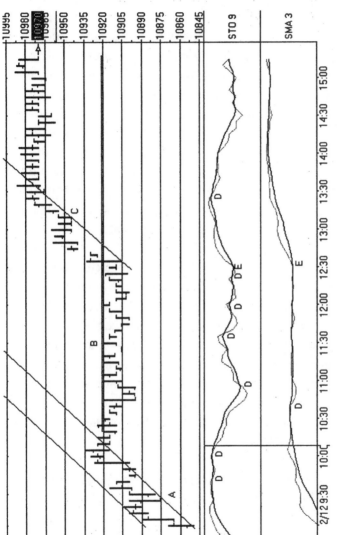

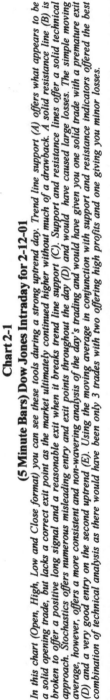

Chart 2-1
(5 Minute Bars) Dow Jones Intraday for 2-12-01

In this chart (Open, High, Low and Close format) you can see these tools during a strong uptrend day. Trend line support (A) offers what appears to be a solid opening trade, but lacks a correct exit point as the market ultimately continued higher without much of a drawback. A solid resistance line (B) is broken to offer a positive long signal and a reasonable exit when it breaks trend line support (C). Support and resistance lines offer a solid technical approach. Stochastics offers numerous misleading entry and exit points throughout the day (D) and would have caused large losses. The simple moving average, however, offers a more consistent and non-wavering analysis of the day's trading and would have given you one solid trade with a premature exit (D) and a very good entry on the second uptrend (E). Using the moving average in conjunction with support and resistance indicators offered the best combination of technical analysis as there would have been only 3 trades with two offering high profits and one giving you minor losses.

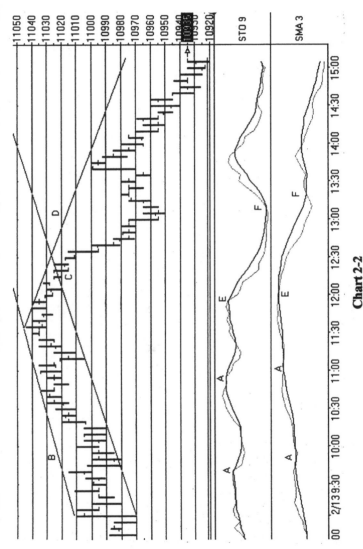

Chart 2-2

(5 Minute Bars) Dow Jones Intraday for 2-13-01

In this chart (Open, High, Low and Close format) you can see the use of all three tools during what would be considered a choppy yet trend based trading day. You would have a difficult time using stochastics or a simple moving average, as they both provide a number of false signals throughout the course of the day. This can be observed early in the day as the initial uptrend is contradicted by numerous sell signals in both tools (A). While both tools offer a reasonable entry point on the reversal (E), they both indicate an incorrect and unnecessary exit (F). The trend lines (support and resistance), however, offer an excellent viewpoint of how to maximize profits on this particular day. Moreover, it should be visible early on in the day that both the simple moving average and stochastics were giving false signals, while the trend lines (or tightening channel) (B) was providing a solid trade, and when the market broke (C) provided an even more profitable short signal without a false exit (D). Also, the trend lines provided clear and concise trailing stops and reversal points. You are able to understand this early in the course of the day and use the scope of daytrading as a time guide for the validity of these tools (as this apparent observation may change tomorrow.)

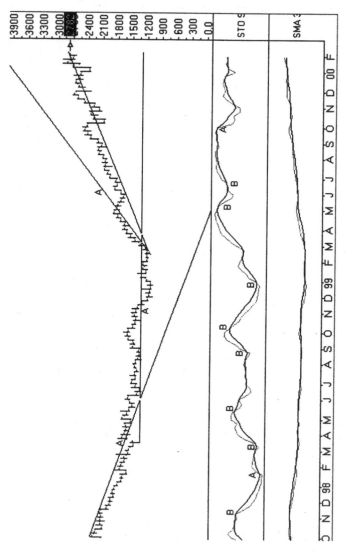

Chart 2-3
Weekly Crude Oil

In this weekly crude oil chart, none of the three trend lines nor the support line (A) offered anything but incorrect signals. Stochastics, however, provided clear and concise entry and exit points (B), with minimal losses (A) on incorrect signals. A market like crude oil can be predicted over the course of several years on a weekly chart using stochastics as an early turning point tool because you have spent the time to analyze the accuracy of a tool over a long history. This simple moving average offers little to comment on as it stays consistently congested and offers few indications of turning points. Realizing this as a tool to ignore in this market over this time frame can save you many mistakes.

If you follow some simple do's and don'ts of technical tools, outlined below, you will be that much closer to becoming an expert trader. Take technical trading with a grain of salt. It works if applied from a perspective that allows distance between you and the micro aspects of the tools you are using. Combine technical and fundamental trading without exception.

Find the technical tools that make sense for the given type of analysis within a given market. Technical tools have application, but not in every market or every time frame. Let history be your guide as to what tools work and which do not. If you do not take the time to research the history of the tools you are using for a given market, you are doomed for failure. If you are daytrading a market, test a tool for as many as 180 days back to discover its ability to predict results consistently and accurately. If you are analyzing daily charts, use two to five years of charting to test the tools. Seasonal and cyclical trends require as much historical evidence as possible, as long as it is accurate to today's market conditions (roughly 20 years or more).

Understand your tools. What is it they are analyzing, and how does that help you to predict price in a given market? Technical trading is not an art: it's a science. Within scientific analysis there is a reason for everything, an explanation for every right and wrong. Learn technical trading from the ground up. If you can teach it to someone else then you can say you have mastered it. Be able to answer why you use it, how to use it properly, when to apply it (over what time frame), which tool to use, and what market to use it for.

Avoid using multiple tools that all have the same general application. A number of tools have similar attributes with slight variations (i.e. MACD, simple and lagging moving averages, etc.), which can often cause a technical trader to over exaggerate the value of these tools and their complimentary signals. If you use multiple tools be able to explain why they are providing complimentary signals, and why they are similar or different.

Simplest is best. Why use a complex tool when a simpler one explains and predicts the same movement? Find the technical trading tools that work best for you. If it doesn't make *perfect* sense, then don't use it.

No fudging. A common mistake when drawing and identifying chart formations and signals is what I like to call fudging your charts. We have all done it before: the head and shoulders pattern that looks more like the head, shoulder and elbow pattern; the trend line support that looks like a roller coaster off its tracks; the Elliott Wave that just doesn't fit. It is a completely understandable human psychological error, but we all try to find patterns whether one is there or not. That's not to say a double bottom wouldn't be one if it were a tick or two off. However, a trader must have scope and be able to take a few steps back to make a rational analysis.

A word on system trading. Are technical indicators the bible by which traders should have their trades dictated? While I do not share this belief, those who do are known as system traders and believe strongly in the sole power of numbers to profit from market movements. What is in a programmed trading system, and why are there so many believers in the power of such systems? Simply, all technical analysis is built on the premise that history repeats itself, so systems are intended to find the historical patterns that have the greatest statistical correlation to a current pattern. They use selected indicators with a high degree of statistical correlation that have historical significance in predicting future results when combined together into one system. A proper system ways time, historical and statistical relevance and accuracy to maximize returns and minimize risk. A large percentage of systems make the mistake of finding statistical correlation among similar indicators and have a system based on a reoccurring signal among indicators that should be giving similar signals. This presents itself as a system that has strong directional signals when in reality it is most likely only taking a small amount of true factors into account. Another mistake of systems is inappropriate time frames. A short term system that does not check historical short term patterns to recognize current ones is bound for failure. Markets tend to go through cycles and fluctuating patterns. If the system shows gains when the market is exhibiting only a couple of patterns and loses when other patterns show themselves, it is most likely using indicators without historical reference. Systems should be back tested for a minimum of five years and in real time trading for at least one year before an investor should bother analyzing the returns of the system. A proper system should have no life span. If they do then they are only taking advantage of a current set of patterns, which is not a true system. When analyzing systems use the outline above of what to avoid and to look for in a system and you will find very few meet these criteria.

SECRET #3
VOLUME CONTROLS EVERYTHING

Fundamentals and technicals; traders spend most of there time overanalyzing these important investment informational tools, but they're not everything. While they can signal market moves and provide solid risk management information, volume is typically an investor's first indicator of future market moves. Moreover, volume can signal upcoming fundamental or technical changes in a market. There are four main types of identifications of volume in a market: static, sporadic, increasing and decreasing.

Static, or flat volume is typically found in markets with no new fundamental or technical changes, with no expected changes in the near future. This is common in markets that are in a trading range or that are steadily trending. A market stuck in a trading range would present an opportunity to be a seller of out of the money puts and calls. While the premiums in these options would be relatively low (unless you identified a static market early on), the strategy would allow you to take advantage of time depreciation in the options during a period of dying volatility and a flat market condition. Following a commitment of traders report for the market prior to taking this strategy would be advisable to avoid investing in a flat market that has an evolving shift of long to short (or vice versa) positions. Most commitment reports can be found on the web at www.usda.gov or at the market's exchange site.

A steadily trending market with static volume would likely indicate a future breakout complemented by a spike in volume just prior to or on the day of the breakout (#3.1). Purchasing puts and calls would be a possible strategy if a volume shift is seen prior to the breakout. The more days of strong volume change prior to the breakout without a return to the static volume range, the better the trade.

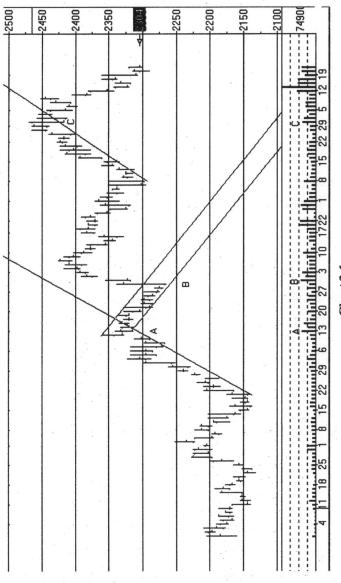

Chart 3-1

Daily July '01 Corn

In this daily chart of corn there are three clear cut examples (A, B & C) of a steadily trending market with static volume spiking just before the breakout from the pattern. Break A illustrates a volume spike ahead of a reversal pattern and breakout of a support line and channel. Break B shows a volume indicator during a breakout. Break C demonstrates a volume spike on the day of the price break.

Sporadic volume can be identified in markets with constantly changing fundamentals, technical breaks, short/long covering, insider information, or upcoming reports. The key to profiting from constantly changing volume in markets is understanding why it is occurring in the first place. Changing fundamentals creates sporadic volume when the fundamentals are unstable and causes a 'batting heads' market environment. Two (or more) opposing viewpoints on the affect of fundamental news, or on what future fundamental changes may occur, cause buyers and sellers to war on direction. Typically, pauses occur (breathers in market fluctuations) and volume dips as the two sides analyze price change versus fundamental viewpoints. This often provides an opportunity to play opposite any market moves as long as the market stays within its recent relative trading range. With the increased level of risk it is recommended to utilize an opposing out of the money option for protection (if going long use a put, and if going short use a call) and for expanding your options (no pun intended) within the trade design. Thus if the market falls back into range making your futures profitable, this trade design would allow you to exit your futures and hold the opposing option to play the other side should the other 'butting head' push the market back in the opposite direction. The trade allows you to control margin and reduce risk while providing a solid opportunity to profit from volatility (what the trade was originally intended for) rather than direction, thereby taking full advantage of the sporadic volume.

Technical breakouts in a market can sometimes cause sporadic volume as the market digests the new movement. If this occurs, one must look at the reasons for the breakout rather than just the technical move. When a volume pause occurs on a technical breakout it means one of two events are occurring in the market. Either the market is reversing or waiting for confirmation to continue the breakout. This can happen when a fundamental change is occurring or when the technical breakout was merely due to unusual circumstances (i.e. large buyer/seller makes a position shift, a large stop area is run through, false rumors, vacation weekend for traders, etc.). This type of volume pause is most likely an indication of a false breakout and should be closely analyzed for news prior to making trading decisions. A solid strategy is to take the opposing side on a futures contract and place a stop beyond the previous high volume day's high (if the breakout was to the upside) or low (if the breakout was to the downside). The contingency is that the day after the breakout (the low volume day) the market must stay within the breakout day's trading range. (#3.2)

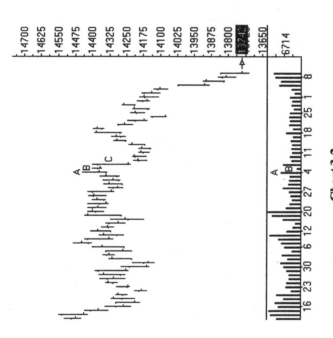

Chart 3-2

Daily June '01 British Pound

For this example, let's look at a daily chart of the British Pound. Point A shows a technical break with a large volume inside day with dramatically lower volume. This gives us a sell signal with a stop above point A's high. As you can see, the following day the strong pullback (C) makes this a profitable trade. Keep in mind that you are using a one day move, followed by a one day volume and price confirmation, so the predicted move should be within a relatively short time frame (a few days).

A short/long covering with volume and price spikes followed by a low volume day would look similar to the technical breakout described above. However, short covering would most likely be an exception to the rule and should be viewed as an indication of an upcoming near term fundamental shift. An indication of this would be found in looking at the back months of the futures contract and finding that the back months had an unusually long delayed reaction to the breakout (intraday). The key to identifying whether it was short/long covering or not is to play close attention to market coverage after the spike trading day ends. Look for analysis of the floor trading which should be a tip off as to whether covering took place rather than stops being hit or large (non-covering) orders coming in. If short/long covering was the reason for the spike it would create some doubts as to whether the breakout was false. Typically, there is a pause during large covering positions as the traders doing the covering attempt to 'calm' the market to avoid adding unnecessary costs by having the market participate in the covering thereby pushing the price against them. So what does all this mean? If short/long covering is the probable reason for the spike, avoid the market as a reversal is less likely, but there is no guarantee of a continued rally.

Insider information can cause sporadic volume as inside market participants attempt to hide their activity. This is certainly difficult to discover as an individual speculator, but there are some tip offs that can help you to figure it out. When insiders get a jump on a market you will often find changes in volume over the course of a number of days as the information slowly leaks out. Most analytical coverage on the market will appear to be worthless and uninformative, with potentially some commentary on individual large trade blocks going through. Stops, short/long covering, and consistencies in daily volume will all be absent from the market for several days. When all of these 'tip-offs' come together, there is most likely some insider trading occurring and should be viewed as an opportunity to jump on the bandwagon. Stop placement below the low of the original spike day (if the spike is to the upside) or above the high (if the spike is to the downside) is a recommended risk management strategy.

Similar to the changing fundamentals scenario, upcoming reports can create a 'butting heads' mentality among market participants as players attempt to predict the future outcome of these reports. As reports, rumors or inside information leak, sporadic volume and price fluctuation can occur until the time of the report. The majority of the time the market has a tendency to return to its original price range as the report approaches. Option premium tends to be the only steady and predictable trading opportunity in this type of scenario. Often, options' premiums steadily increase as the report nears and question still remains, making a breakout following the report more and more probable. Buying puts and calls (strangling or straddling the market) during this sporadic trading and exiting just prior to the report is a safe play and carries a high probability of profit. Holding through the report is not a bad strategy, although it certainly carries a higher level of risk (#3.3).

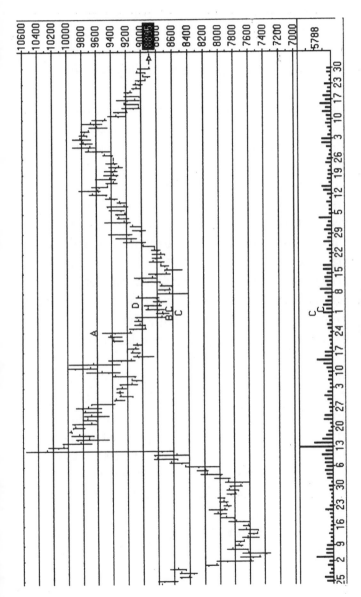

Chart 3-3

Daily Orange Juice for Oct '99

Going into the historically volatile October 5th crop report, a long NTM (near the money) strangle (i.e. long 90 call & long 85 put, 1 to 1, with the market near 88) can be a profitable strategy at times. Being aware of option premiums, however, can often be the key to identifying if it is in fact a good trade. Low volume in the prior week's trading helped a dramatic drop in prices (A to B). This was followed by two high volume days heading into the report as speculators adjusted their positions (C). Option premiums on the strangle mentioned above (which expired at the end of the week) went from less than 3 points ($450) to over 8 points ($1200) just on the two day volume spike prior to the report (despite losing over 30% of the remaining time value). The day of the report (D) became a relatively flat day, as the expected volatile price action was dulled by a benign report. Option volatility, which was at an extreme high going into the report, dropped to practically nothing, and the missing time value depreciation instantly came back into the option prices. A $1200 NTM strangle, purchased near the close of the day prior to the report, was now worth around $200 within an hour of the open the following day. The right trade, when properly identifying the excessive volatility premium, would have been to sell the strangle or a condor (a strangle with protection).

Sporadic volume normally carries sporadic price movements with it, and creates confusing chart patterns and fundamental question marks. Therefore, an investor must research the reasons behind the sporadic movements to maximize probability of profit.

Increasing or decreasing volume is most notably found in markets with changing technicals, new fundamentals, upcoming reports, and insider and fund buying. Increasing volume is a sign of increasingly stronger opinions, as more and more speculators enter the market for the reasons given above. If a direction is complemented by increasing volume over a number of days, the increasing volume indicator would be a confirmation of the move. Conversely, decreasing volume would be a sign of a 'weak' move and would signal a potential upcoming reversal. The general rule of thumb is that a technical breakout with increasing volume is a sound breakout, while a breakout with decreasing volume is a warning sign of a false move. Low volume on a breakout followed by a high volume confirmation (rare) is a very strong sign of a confirmed breakout.

Steadily increasing volume during or after fundamental change, regardless of price change, will increase market volatility and offer opportunities to be a seller of options as put and call premiums become excessive. These increased call premiums must be weighted against true market volatility rather than inherently increasingly volatility within the options. Quite often option volatility exceeds market volatility during times of increasing volume, which can create great opportunities to play covered call and put spreads. This strategy takes advantage of the excessive option premiums by being a seller of those options, while providing protection and a direction picking opportunity.

Constantly decreasing volume during or after fundamental change generally means one of two events are occurring: the market believes the news is out and market participants have priced the market within a trading range, or the market 'calms' ahead of additional news. The key is to know which one is causing the declining volume. The first provides an opportunity to sell out of the money puts and calls (strangles), while the latter creates a buying opportunity (long strangle/straddle) if option premiums drop as time decay and dying volatility provide good pricing ahead of future volatility.

Continually increasing volume ahead of upcoming reports adds volatility to the market, and premium to the options. The market is positioning themselves ahead of the unknown, which would normally create sporadic volume, but can sometimes create steadily increasing volume and thus different trading opportunities. If this is the case, the market is generally not expecting any changes between now and the upcoming report, and is simply increasing their 'pace' as the report grows nearer. This build up most often comes before an explosive volume and price move following the report. Therefore, the best strategy to take is ratio spreading options (although long straddles, strangles, and covered futures positions make solid trade ideas as well) which essentially means selling one nearby option to collect premium and buying two or more farther out of the money options. This exploits a directional trade ahead of a big move, while protecting cost, margin and risk should your direction be wrong.

Continually decreasing, or 'dead' volume ahead of a report is not as common and is typically found in markets where the report's information is in general universal agreement among market participants. Unfortunately, many traders fall into the trap of finding cheap options and technical indicators suggesting a breakout (a channel for example) and thinking that probability of a move following the report exceeds their cost or risk. If steadily decreasing volume is seen heading into to a 'big' report, do not be fooled; avoid technical indicators and buying options - this is almost always a trap! The market occasionally gets caught off guard, but these times are few and far between.

Insider and fund buying that create a constant increase in volume is generally a confirmation that the market technicals and overall price move is legitimate. Remember, these people know more than you. If a CEO bought two million shares of his own stock in one year after 14 years of buying 100,000 shares every year, don't you think that he knows something you don't? This is not to say that this is by any means a guarantee, but it is a solid piece of confirming information. So, how do you know if funds and insiders are positioning themselves in a market? Identical to conditions in a sporadic volume market, most analytical coverage on the market will appear to be worthless and uninformative, with potentially some commentary on individual large trade blocks going through. Stops, short/long covering, and consistencies in daily volume will all be absent from the market for several days. The difference is that more people know, or a general euphoria from expert agreement in interpreting the market fundamentals cause a universal buying frenzy, but leaves the individual speculator in the dark. These conditions often coincide with the lack of a clear opportunity to join the merry bandwagon (the market pause never occurs).

Clearly, using volume indicators allow traders to identify what is causing most market moves, as well as how to interpret them. If you utilize these indicators with your fundamental and technical analysis you will find it easier to locate trading opportunities in almost any market environment.

SECRET #4
CATCHING THE BREAKOUT

Catching a breakout is the aspiration of all true traders. To most traders, the breakout represents hindsight, could haves and should haves, an afterthought and a fantasy land they only assume they can aspire to reach. To some traders it represents the golden accomplishment, the slaying of the mighty beast. To catch a breakout and ride it from start to finish is a rare find. A dream for most, but an attainable goal for those who follow some simple rules and easy techniques. Imagine catching the recent crude oil run from $11 to $33, or the soybean "beans to the teens" run of 1988, or even the silver breakout to $50 an ounce. This chapter will show you the secret methods for finding and riding the breakout, and some keys to avoiding false signals.

The single most important rule to catching a breakout is having your fundamentals match your technicals. Quite often a trader will see a price break through support or resistance but not have the fundamental change necessary to compliment a continued move. While technical indicators can sometimes suggest a breakout ahead of fundamental change, the possibility of such a fundamental shift is always present.

This book is all about making you, the trader, ask yourself questions to give you perspective. Everything in commodities has a reason, finding it is up to you. This is more critical to finding and taking advantage of breakouts than anything you will learn. Look at long term charts, historical fundamentals, and current price and volume patterns and you will have the scope necessary to identify breakouts. The previous three chapters were intended to give you the understanding of fundamental, technical and volume characteristics and lessons of a given market, all of which are necessary in order to catch a breakout.

In order to successfully catch a breakout and avoid the fakes, a trader must always have a full grasp of fundamental and technical history. Those who focus on the micro present day aspects of the market consistently miss breakouts, and typically get caught playing the other side when the market price gets distorted. Breakouts always have one notable event in common: market hysteria. Time after time a breakout is started with a technical move confirmed by a fundamental shift of future supply and demand. What makes a breakout a breakout is the hysteria or craze that overcomes market participants. Whether it was the bean rally to $11 a bushel in '88 or silver's run to $50 an ounce, they all have present within them a market mentality of limitless potential and a complete lack of negative sentiment. "Irrational exuberance", as Greenspan may have coined it, is what is present in a market breakout that allows it to take that next step to extremes. When the breakout ends the result is almost always a quick and painful retracement to normal levels. This 'market deflation' can sometimes be an even more profitable play than the breakout itself. The following examples are intended to illustrate the grasp of a market a master trader must have to catch a breakout, and sometimes the inevitable retracement.

In 1988 soybeans had an historic breakout with a move from $6 to $11 (refer to chart #4.1, Point B). This constitutes a move of $25,000 or over 2000% on a single contract (estimated margin requirements) in less then four months! Believe it or not, the signs were there long before the breakout ever happened. Since mid-1983 soybeans had bean in a horrible bear climate, with large inventories and ideal weather preventing the market from mounting any type of rally. Prior to the rally, the USDA had put in place a landmark program called the CRP (Conservation Reserve Program). This program improved old systems for reducing soybean supply by limiting the acreage that grains could be planted throughout the US. Moreover, this acreage was held for ten years and the government paid the farmers in cash to create a win-win situation. Slowly, as inventories and supply dwindled, the soybean market formed a bottom. Interestingly, wheat (a substitutive commodity) formed a bottom a few months earlier, an early sign of a market reversal.

What sparked the breakout was one of worst droughts in history, but a master trader saw it coming long before that. Months prior to the drought, a technical break was seen in the market (refer to chart 4.1, Point A). A dead market in 1988 would have marked the fifth consecutive year without helpful weather or positive shifts in supply or demand. This was comparable to the longest depressed prices seen in beans since the CBOT created a contract for it. Moreover, the CRP signaled the beginning of a fundamental shift that was only complemented by the timing of the drought. The drought itself was fast and furious and created hysteria in the market to such great magnitudes that it has rarely been witnessed in history. A record number of limit moves, complemented by the notion that we would literally run out of beans, gave the market all it needed to go through the roof.

The market broke down almost as quickly as it ran up, especially after the market realized they would in fact have enough supply to meet demand. The market was back below $8 within a month, and below the original mark of $6 within a year. This critical short time frame to realize the market had reached a top was signaled by the end of a positive fundamental change. While it may have been psychologically difficult to short beans at $10 or $11 a bushel when it seemed as if it had unlimited upside, the fundamental and historic technical make up of the market confirmed that a top had been reached. (refer to chart #4.1, Point C)

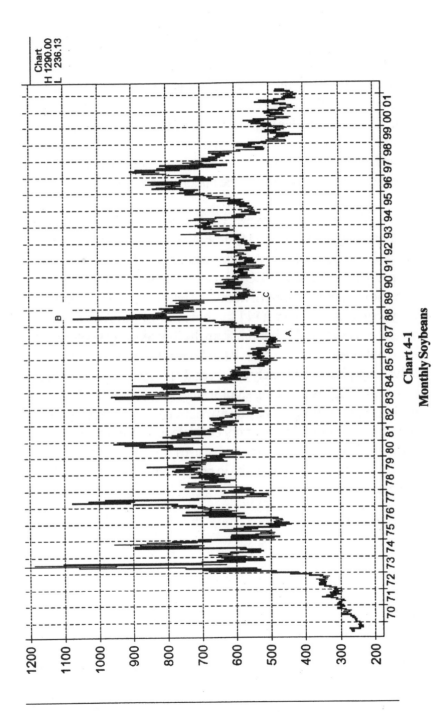

Chart 4-1
Monthly Soybeans

In February of 1999 crude began its own historical run as it tripled in price in just over a year. This mega move meant potential profits of over $20,000, or more then 1000% return on a single contract! Yet again, the signs were there before the market ever hit a bottom. A grasp of the historic fundamental and technical background of the crude market would have been more than enough for a master trader to have caught the majority of the breakout.

Trading at $11 a barrel, crude was well below profitable production levels (estimated to be around $18 a barrel) and seemingly on the brink of worldwide oversupply. The lack of control over supply issues led OPEC to create a retention plan that would have the market involved in a whirlwind rally for two years. Historically, crude hadn't been at $11 for thirteen years and that low was almost a perfect double bottom from the low seen right before this breakout (Please refer to chart #4.2, Points A and B). Fundamentally, supply issues had rarely ever been this severe, and the political power of OPEC was getting significantly stronger over time. The commercials and hedgers were overwhelmingly long, while the specs were caught short. This is a very consistent commonality within breakout markets. A master trader uses this macro view of the market to identify an opportunity to profit from a market's breakout signals. (#4.2)

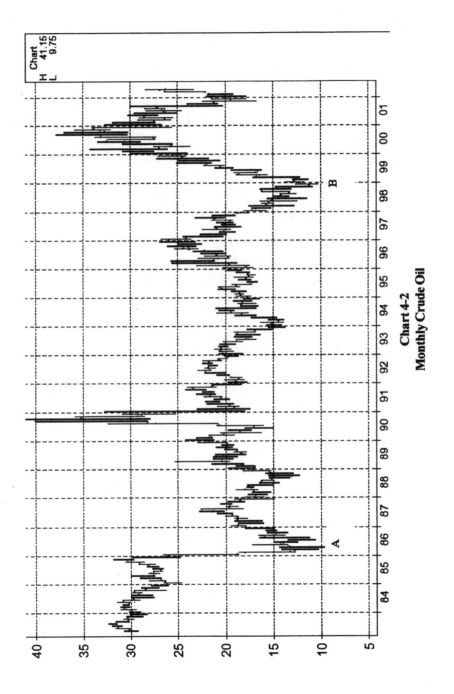

Chart 4-2
Monthly Crude Oil

Relatively thin markets tend to offer some of the most incredible breakouts and retracements ever seen in commodities. Markets like lumber and palladium represent thin markets with a singular fundamental element that consistently causes major shifts in price. While it would take a psychic to be capable of being ahead of such fundamental shifts in these markets, it only takes a knowledge of history to jump on these moves early and stay for the ride.

Palladium has a fundamental history that revolves around questionable supply practices of Russia, which supplies around 70% of the world's palladium. With little to no notice of supply shortages, palladium is known for some of the most outrageous price moves in history. This lack of fundamental predictability leaves a trader to identify a breakout through technical and volume studies. These thin markets tend to come back down just as fast as they run up, so using historical prices to determine when to exit long and go short is the single most important tool in playing both sides of the breakout. (#4.3)

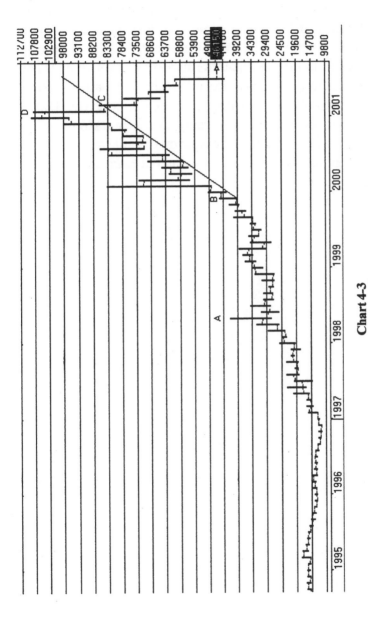

Chart 4-3
Monthly Palladium

Here you can see the most recent breakout of palladium, sparked by news of heavily declining inventories in Russia, as well as increased demand. When the market broke through (B) a previous monthly spike high (A), a buy signal was given. The market then followed trend line support from that breakout (C) to massive highs. A strong sell signal was given when the market crashed through that support after a failed attempt at breaking the new highs (D).

Similarly, lumber is a thin market with the capability of fundamental shifts that turn on a dime. While demand tends to be identifiable and typically cyclical in nature, supply is a relative question mark and sometimes takes the market by storm. A constant observance of long term historical prices allows a master trader to use this macro outlook to identify pivot points in which market reversals tend to occur. More importantly, such technical observance would allow a trader to spot a breakout on an initial move, as typically lumber follows through on breakouts once a given percentage move occurs. (#4.4)

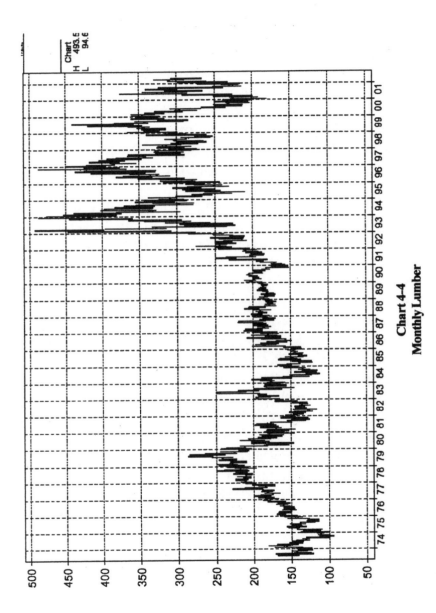

Chart 4-4
Monthly Lumber

How do these examples differ from markets that fake a breakout? The majority of the time it is the failure of a market to follow through with the expected fundamental shift that stalls a breakout. However, the warning signs are there, and the reality is that even a master trader will participate in market moves that ultimately do not complete a breakout. The secret is to be able to identify the lack of a breakout confirmation as early as possible. The master trader will have specific rules to exit markets when key signals indicate a breakout or lack thereof.

In thin markets, avoid using exact technical indicators for stop placement and entry points. Room must be left for excessive movement when an influx of orders push a market towards these technical points. Thin markets are most susceptible to spikes and skewed intraday patterns. In more heavily traded markets tighter stops and entry points can be used. A breakout is generally a fluid market move. It appears that retracements never complete themselves and it is almost impossible to find a good entry point. This is a good thing. It provides validity and confirmation to the trading taking place. If entry point is difficult because your stop would have to be too far away, then use an opposing at or near the money option for protection. This simple technique is often overlooked, and can be a most valuable method for playing breakouts. It provides unlimited upside, while defining risk and margin. Most importantly, it eliminates the need for a futures stop, thus increasing the probability of the trade working because of the ability to stay in the market. Moreover, these options typically have less premium than the opposite option because the market is going in the other direction.

If emotion enters into a trade, it is almost always doomed for failure. If ever there is a chance for this to occur, it is during a possible breakout. Risk management is the single most important element to avoid getting caught in a 'fakeout'. Any trader will fall into 'fakeouts' when they continually attempt to catch a breakout, but a master trader will take minimal losses by utilizing some simple risk management techniques.

The methods for maximizing the probability and profitability of breakouts, while minimizes risk and loss is a difficult combination of proper trade application and risk management techniques. You have just learned the recognition techniques necessary to become a master trader. The following three chapters are intended to illustrate the proper application of these techniques through trade design and risk management approaches.

SECRET #5
RISK MANAGEMENT; UNDERSTANDING WHY YOU DO WHAT YOU DO

Risk management, the science of controlling risk exposure while maximizing profitability, is a vital piece to becoming a master trader. Imagine having the exposure to profit from leveraged markets without having the same exposure to losses. This is the idea behind risk management. This chapter exposes the do's and don'ts and the secrets behind successful risk management.

If used properly, risk management is the counterattack to emotion. Knowing when to take gains and when to accept losses is one of the most difficult aspects of being a master trader. A trader must, without exception, predetermine the entry and exit strategy of each and every trade *prior* to entering into a market. If you use this rule you have already overcome the biggest obstacle a trader encounters. This is the obstacle of emotion.

When you predetermine entry into a market you need to identify the trade's intention, the potential risk and the expected reward. Ask yourself why you are entering into the trade. Is it fundamental, technical, volume driven or a combination of the three?

Your entry point should compliment your rationale for entering the market. When you predetermine exit strategy out of a market you need to identify the trade's intention, associated risks and profit maximizing goals. The exit strategy should also compliment your rationale for entering into the market. The following examples are intended to bring the rationale to the forefront of entry and exit point decision making. Keep in mind that these are examples of thought process and not the *only* way to approach proper risk management techniques.

For our first example, let's take a look at the crude oil breakout discussed in chapter 4 (please refer to charts 2.4 and 4.2). As the market approached a near perfect technical double bottom dating back to 1986, a technical buy signal developed. Keep in mind the fundamental rationale we discussed about crude oil at the time the market was reaching the $10 level. Because changing fundamentals have caused a 'batting heads' trading environment, sporadic volume is quite visible. As we learned in chapter 3, when the sporadic volume calms down, typically during sideways or range bound trading, it provides an opportune time to play opposite the recent market move. So here we have a fundamental, technical and volume rationale that would make any master trader drool over the opportunity. Given these circumstances, an appropriate trade design would be to enter the market with long futures (preferably more than one), with a generous stop well below 1986's low, or purchase an out-of-the-money put for protection in place of the stop. We want a large cushion because the trade is designed to take advantage of a long term reversal with the expectation for large gains over time. Therefore, a master trader would give himself a fairly large stop out cushion to increase the probability of staying in the trade. You may be asking yourself why it is recommended to use more than one futures contract. The market is not going to go straight up. If you have called the bottom and breakout correctly, then the market should still experiences spikes in both directions as it trends upwards. Keep in mind how long it took the market to get down to these prices in the first place. Using more than one contract allows you to maintain a base quantity of contracts that will always be long the market (so as to avoid missing any moves to the upside), while having additional contracts to exit on spike rallies, and buy back on dips.

In our second example, we look at a T-Bond (30yr) market that had been in steady decline for a year and four months. This drop ultimately amounted to a move worth over $22,000 on a single contract (or over 1100%)! Picking a bottom in a market like this would be a feat for even the very best traders, but legitimate signs of a reversal were there. Looking at chart 5.1, you can see the technical rationale to buying into the market

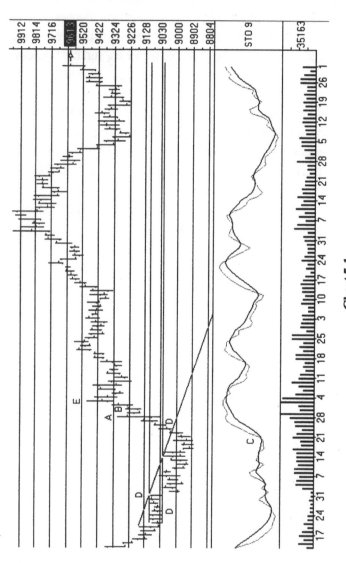

Chart 5-1

Daily 30 yr. T-Bond for beginning of '00

Note: During periods of expected rises in volatility one should always look for opportunities to buy strangles and straddles as a valid trade idea if you do not have a gauge on direction. During periods of expected decreases in volatility one should always look for opportunities to sell strangles and straddles as a valid trade idea if you do not have a gauge on direction. Keep in mind the defined risk of buying versus the unlimited risk of selling.

Forgetting the enormous drop already seen in the market, the downtrend started to appear to be coming to an end when light volume led to sideways trading. After an apparent bottoming out formation developed (stochastics, point C on chart 5.1), high volume entered the market ahead of the Feb. 2nd FOMC report and pushed the market through numerous resistance points (points D on chart 5.1). Just before the report the market spiked well above nearby resistance (point A on chart 5.1), and signaled a confirmed buy a couple of days after the report (point B) on another spike high (point E on chart 5.1). Fundamentally, the market was turning despite continued Fed policy of interest rates. However, the market had clearly over-estimated the expected length of the Fed's raising rates tendency and when the market acknowledged a slowing and ultimate upcoming change in policy, the market adjusted. Because of the similarities to the crude oil example in risk exposure, exhaustive downside price action for an extended period, one would think the trading strategy would remain the same. However, the lack of true volatility and declining value of call options, a ratio bull call spread would offer the lowest risk opportunity to capitalize on a reversal. Moreover, this example doesn't provide for any type of legitimate stop placement on a futures contract. By utilizing a relatively long term ratio bull call spread (i.e. Short 1 near-the-money call, long 3 or 4 out of the money calls, 2 to 3 months out), risk is defined, costs are minimized and upside exposure is tremendous.

The key to stop placement is utilizing stops to allow for a proper exit to a market or a better reentry point. Too often traders use stops as an ultimate exit strategy to a futures contract, but a master trader sometimes will use it as a reversal point or a pause before reentering at a better price. Stops are technical points that represent a psychological support or resistance level. In macro stop placement, whereas a trader maintains a broader and more long term perspective, the stop is chosen at a price point that indicates a major fundamental shift in the market's perception of supply and/or demand. This can sometimes indicate an opportunity to reverse your position should proper risk management techniques present themselves in the market. In micro stop placement, whereas a trader maintains a confined short term market outlook, the stop is generally used to gauge buying or selling pressure, or lack thereof, holding a support or resistance area. This can sometimes indicate not only an opportunity to reverse, but can also indicate an opportunity to reenter at a better price when a new or historical point of support or resistance is seen. If you are placing a stop for another reason, with little exception, you are placing your stops incorrectly.

For a master trader, exact stop placement is a difficult and complex combination of understanding the market's historic technical and fundamental history and the market's current price, volume and volatility characteristics. This comprehension allows a master trader the ability to rationalize and justify specific stop placement. Chapters one through three explained how to properly gain comprehension and perspective in a given market's historic and current fundamental, technical and volume characteristics. The application of stop placement given this understanding is individual to the market, but becomes common sense and self-explanatory when this level of knowledge is achieved.

Fundamentally speaking, have an acute awareness of a market's supply and demand structure. Weather markets tend to have technical breaks during periods of changing fundamentals (or potential changes) that distort clear technical stop placement. This often causes a trader to want to reenter a market as soon as they're stopped out due to whipsaw price action at, near and through support or resistance levels. If you are playing a weather market for a seasonal breakout, a stop is not always the wise approach. An option covering your futures allows for time, instead of price, to control the success of the trade. This is most often the logical approach since weather implications on a market typically only exist for a brief and specific period of time throughout a given year. If you need to use a stop instead of an opposing option, then make sure to predefine reentry into the market so as to avoid the emotional pitfalls of such an approach.

Stop placement requires mastery of technical analysis. Moreover, the mastery of a technical history of a market is critical because of the need for understanding what chart patterns hold and follow through in a specific market. I believe stop placement is very visual when you get past the knowledge. Visualize the continuation of chart patterns over time. Look at as many charts as possible, covering as many time periods as possible. This can only compliment your research and knowledge.

As discussed in the breakouts chapter, it is critical to determine the volume and open interest in determining both macro and micro stop placement. Perhaps more relevant in micro stop placement, thin markets require larger cushions and spacing with stops in relation to support or resistance.

An often overlooked aspect to stop placement is whether the market's core trading is speculative, hedging or derivative in nature. A speculative market, for instance gold or the dollar, is based mainly on the speculative interest and is the primary trade for that market. The volume traded in a speculative market is almost always greater than in its cash trade. It tends to make numerous common technical formations and often shows unique buying or selling price points. Typically, these are markets that are technically driven and stop placement appears to be an easy decision. Historically, these markets often break through price support and resistance levels before ultimately resuming the trend. These markets also tend to be driven by floor trading and often use obvious stop points as targets in order to create trading opportunities, volume and price action. Therefore, in these markets one should avoid tight stops and seek out less obvious support and resistance points. More complex technical patterns (head shoulders, flags, MACD, Bollinger Bands, etc.) tend to have the greatest amount of success.

A hedging market, for instance cattle or crude oil, is based on the producer interest and is generally a secondary market behind cash trade. These markets tend to hold long term support and resistance and short term trend lines. It is key to identify breaks in these support and resistance levels as it is generally a strong indicator of changes in market sentiment and future trends in hedging markets. These markets also have a sensitivity to regular reports and forecasts of fundamental and cash price shifts. Reentry and scaling stop techniques are often the most successful ways to trade these markets.

A derivative market, for instance the S&P 500 or the CRB index, have elements of hedging and speculation, but differ from other markets in that they are based on movements from multiple markets that have a commonality. When it comes to stop placement in these markets it is mostly technically driven, since the fundamental nature is complex and difficult. It is important to identify if these derivatives are in a pattern of trading ahead, with or behind the physical markets, as this will provide keen insight into proper stop placement. These markets tend to require loose stops as technically driven markets frequently drive through visible levels of support and resistance only to ultimately reverse. Volume also makes a large impact in volatility in these markets. The less volume, the more market trades outside of its 'true' range, and the wider the stops.

The idea of stop placement based on monetary drawbacks has always been an absurd concept to me. Do you enter into your trades because of the monetary drawback? Then why would you exit for that reason? There are a million trades in given market in a given day, but the trades that maximize risk management are the ones that take the least possible loss with the highest probability of a potential reward over time. If you have a strong belief that a market will go in a given direction, but lack a technical stop placement that stays within the level of risk you are comfortable with for that particular trade, then don't place the trade. Or, enter the market with an opposing option instead of a stop, or with just options. Futures represent only one method of entering into a market; there are other ways to extract the identical or similar performance in the market without utilizing futures, but that allow risk management to stay within your overall objectives.

The trailing stop is a vital element to risk management. It provides the trader the ability to adjust to technical shifts in the market, lock in profits, and protect losses. The common mistake with trailing stops is that traders use them simply to trail profits, when in fact a trailing stop should be used as a complementary technique to your original rationale for entering the trade. A trailing stop is often overused because it presents a reasonable middle ground between emotional risk taking and exiting a trade entirely. A trailing stop should only be used if a new and desirable trade presents itself. Ask yourself, if I entered this trade today, where would my stop be and why? If the answer shows itself to be a mismanaged trade idea, then a trailing stop is not the answer. A trailing stop is most applicable in daytrading environments and in markets that have more then one point of support or resistance within the framework of a trade's price target.

Allow me to address the market's tendency to appear as if they are gunning for your stop. The 'catch 22' to technical analysis is that a clear chart pattern is clear to anyone who looks at it. So, if everyone puts their stops in the same place because they are all looking at the same chart, then you have a bunch of stops at the same point. I like to call this the Ken Roberts phenomenon. You have all these traders following one method for entry and stop placement so that the market has no choice but to inevitably pressure this price support or resistance. It is commonplace, especially in thin markets, to gravitate towards the direction of the largest order volume. It presents profit opportunities for those who are aware of these price points, and the floor traders always seek out additional volume and volatility. They're not gunning for your stops, they're gunning for volume. Take this with a grain of salt though, because support is support and resistance is resistance. It becomes a matter of does the buying pressure exceed the selling pressure, hence the battle over support or resistance. The lesson here is that a master trader needs to be aware of stop placement in respect to the rest of the market.

Scaling in and out of multiple positions with stops is an often overlooked form of risk management. In markets where support and resistance lie in a number of reasonable places to put a stop, it thereby creates an opportunity to scale into and out of a market.

There are a number of ways to avoid monetary stops using options. As I have mentioned a number of times throughout "7 Secrets", utilizing opposing options to protect your futures position, in place of stops, can yield a greater probability of profit with defined risk exposure. The downside to this type of strategy is that your futures contract has to overcome the cost of the option to achieve profitability, versus a futures contract needs to simply go in your favor to create a winning trade. The upside is that the market can move outside of where your stop placement would be and still become a winning trade because the option allowed you to remain in the market. The pro's and con's to this strategy give clear parameters on when to use it:

- When you are entering a market without clearly definable support or resistance
- When you are entering a market for an ultimate price move, but entry point is difficult
- When you are entering a market with extreme volatility, gap opens, or upcoming reports
- When you are playing a seasonal weather breakout
- When you want to scale into a market over a large price range
- When you are using it in place of a trailing stop or when not to use it:
- When proper risk management can be achieved using stops
- When trade design requires only a small price move
- When option spreads present better trade definition than this strategy (Chapter 7)
- When the trade's intention is take advantage of a specific point of support or resistance

Risk management is one of the most difficult skills a master trader attains, but critical to eliminating emotion and creating consistency in trading. Grasping risk, reward and probability prior to entering into a market only furthers the principles of risk management by applying it to trade design.

SECRET #6
RISK, REWARD AND PROBABILITY

When I am asked how I devise my trading strategies, whether I utilize fundamentals, technicals, or volume as my primary guide, the response is none of the above. There are thousands of trading opportunities in a given trading day, but the trades I take advantage of are the ones that require the least amount of risk with the greatest amount of potential profit over time. Moreover, it is essential to have a maximizing combination of risk, reward and probability. Specifically, the risk being the potential loss, the reward being the potential gain, and the probability being the percentage chance of potential gains or losses. This type of trade analysis falls into two categories: futures and options.

Let's look at a simple example of the net result of this type of analysis on a futures contract. If you bought a crude oil contract at $20 a barrel. Your stop loss was placed at $15, and profit exit is at $25. At $10 per 1-cent move in a crude contract, your risk is $5,000 and your reward is also $5,000. Since both targets are equidistant from your entry point, your probability of loss is 50% as is your probability of gain. Seems simple enough, right? Now let's say that you bought the contract at $20, but your stop was at $18 and your profit target was at $24. Your risk then becomes $2,000, and your reward changes to $4,000. Your probability of loss is 66.67%, while your probability of gain is 33.33%. This is calculated simply based on the difference between the percentage chance of the necessary price move to achieve loss versus the price move necessary to achieve the gain. In this instance, the reward of $4,000 requires twice the price move of the $2,000 risk (on a percentage basis, it computes to 66.67% versus 33.33%; half the probability of one versus the other). This means that theoretically this trade should get stopped out two times for every time you hit your profit target.

Now that you understand how to compute probability of risk and reward within a futures trade, it is important to realize that there are an unlimited amount of variables that can interfere with this seemingly easy equation. Something as simple as a trailing stop or volatility spikes in a market, gap and limit moves, and so on, can make it nearly impossible to achieve specific probability calculations. Nevertheless, it is a key function of a master trader's trade design to properly assess these factors and derive at a meaningful probability of risk and reward. I recommend approaching this type of analysis by utilizing a few of the plethora of price and volatility probability calculators that are widely available in financial analysis software. A simple price probability program will take a given amount of historical price movement and allow you to input the current price and anticipated price move over a given period of time. It will then compute the percentage likelihood of a given price target being hit over a given time frame by using historical price moves to compute probability. This will provide valuable insight into stop placement and risk/reward strategies, and is a vital tool when analyzing options and option spreads. While this is certainly not an exact science, it provides an avenue to approach trade design, and to eliminate emotion in not only the act of trading but in the act of designing a trade.

When approaching options with this type of trade analysis, delta computation provides tremendous insight into probability of different risk and reward scenarios. Countless books have been written on delta analysis, so to explain it in full detail in a page or two would be futile. However, understanding what it means and how to apply it to probability analysis is simple. Delta, a number between 0 and 1.00, is a measure of the percentage change in price of an option for every point move in the underlying futures contract. So, if you bought a $25 crude oil call for $100 with crude futures at $20, and the option had a delta of .2, then a move in the futures to $21 would theoretically make the option worth $300 ($1,000 [futures move] X .2 [delta] = $200 + $100 [original value of the call] = $300). The difficulty in this type of analysis is that delta changes as the futures price moves closer or farther away from the strike price of the option. This is known as gamma. Gamma is a measure of a how quickly delta changes for every point move in the underlying futures contract. As a general rule, as the futures market moves closer to an out of the money option, the delta increases, and as it moves farther away from a strike price, the delta of the option decreases. Exceptions occur when volatility and other factors affect option premiums.

Delta and gamma apply to probability analysis of options by allowing the trader to assess gains or losses over time as compared to a move in the underlying futures price. What is the probability of the success or failure of an option? You can determine this by ascertaining the necessary price move in a futures contract, times that by the delta of the option (factoring in gamma over the course of the price move), minus time value depreciation to achieve your profit target in your option (or for that matter using this calculation to determine the probability of hitting your loss/exit target). Probability and option calculators can often be programmed to make these calculations for you. Over time, a master trader becomes very familiar with hypothetical probability analysis and ultimately can estimate this type of calculation to weed out poor probability trades.

While this type of analysis provides valuable insight into futures and option trade designs, the true value to probability analysis is seen when applied to the design of option spreads. Option spreading is the science (and art) of incorporating multiple options to achieve definition in trade design. While chapter 7 goes into detail on why, how and when a master trader uses option spreads, what the following will show you is how to properly apply probability analysis to this valuable trading methodology. For the sake of learning by example, let's look at an option spread strategy and how one would approach probability analysis.

Crude futures are at $25. You purchase one crude oil $25.00 call for $1,500, and sell three $28.00 calls for $700 each, or $2,100 total. There are 80 days to expiration on both options. This call ratio spread would put a net credit of $600 into your account because you received $600 more for the options you sold then the cost of the one you bought (6.1). When performing this type of analysis on option spreads, it is best to treat them as European options (to look at profit and loss scenarios based on option prices at expiration), then add in scenarios that take into account time value prior to expiration. At expiration, loss occurs if the futures market is trading above $29.80 (6.2). Loss is $20 per point above $29.80 (due to the ratio of one long call to three short calls, all of which are in the money/intrinsic, creates the equivalent of two short futures at $10 per cent move each, thus $20 per cent move total). Profit scenarios are a bit more complex. $600 profit is achieved if the futures market is below $25.00 at option expiration (6.3), and an additional profit of $10 per cent above $25.00 up to $28.00 (due to the $25 call being intrinsic and the $28 calls being out of the money). Maximum profit is achieved at expiration with the futures contract trading at $28.00, and would be a total profit of $3,600 (6.4). Profit decreases by $20 per cent above $28.00 until $29.80 on the futures (breakeven) (due to the ratio of one long call to three short calls, all of which are in the money/intrinsic). As far as time value prior to expiration, generally speaking, time value works for you as expiration nears with the market below $28.00, while time value would work against you should the market be at, near or slightly above $28.00 prior to expiration.

6.1 $2,100 [credit received by selling 3 $28 calls for $700 each] - $1,500 [cost of $25 call] = $600 [net credit received]

6.2 $4,800 [profit on $25 call] + $600 [credit received on trade] = $5,400 - $5,400 [loss on short options] = $0 or breakeven at $29.80]

6.3 $2,100 [profit on expired worthless $28 calls] - $1,500 [cost of $25 call] = $600 [net profit]; essentially the net credit on the trade is achieved because all options expired worthless

6.4 $3,000 [value of $25 call] + $600 [net credit received] - $0 [value of short $28 calls] = $3600 [net profit at expiration if futures are at $28.00]

Now that you have a sense of the risk and reward scenarios, as well as the influence of time value on this trade design, you can proceed to use the futures and options probability analysis you learned at the very beginning of this chapter. Use a price probability calculator to ascertain the percentage chance that various price targets could be hit. What is the likelihood that, at expiration, the futures would be between $25 and $28, below $25, above $28, and above $29.80? Because this type of trade carries unlimited risk and defined reward, it is very common to have probability on your side. That is, it will be significantly more likely that this trade will yield a profit rather than a loss, as risk is greater than reward. What probability analysis reveals is that while loss is unlimited and can exceed the potential reward, the probability of gains is far greater than the probability of losses. The exact figures could only be determined at the time of the trade, and therefore this only represents an outline on how to approach analyzing option spreads. What I am trying to teach you is that by properly breaking down your trade design you can achieve clarity about the probability of success or failure that would be impossible to identify otherwise. It should be clear that even just understanding the rough outline of probability of trade design allows a master trader to find the trade design that represents the best possible combination of risk, reward and probability for your expected market move.

It is important to note that risk, reward and probability is a give and take relationship. If one element of risk, reward or probability is changed, then the other elements will change accordingly. The interrelationships of these three elements of trade design are vital to understanding their value. In a futures trade analysis, the risk, reward and probability scenarios will always equal themselves out. That is to say:
If X = The risk of any futures trade; Y = The reward of any futures trade
      ZX = The % probability of risk (.01 to 1.00); ZY = The % probability of reward
Then: $ZX = X / (X + Y)$; $ZY = Y / (X + Y)$; $ZX + ZY = 1.00$; $X * ZX = Y * Z$

Option analysis is quite a different story. Because options are derivatives, their pricing is based on both the elements of the option itself and on the elements of the underlying futures contract. This allows for the potential distortion of pricing as applied to risk, reward and probability. Options, for the most part, do not follow the general equation of $ZX + ZY = 1.00$, and therefore can present trading opportunities that futures contracts cannot. If option pricing is skewed from normal probability, spreading options, or simply buying (undervalued) or selling (overvalued) options often maximize the value of using this type of analysis to locate trades that increase your probability of success.

More important than specific examples, probability analysis of different option spread strategies gives a trader an education in designing these complex, but valuable, trades. If you spend the time to understand what each spread design represents, in regards to probability, then you can seek out the markets and options that maximize a risk, reward and probability combination for a particular option spread design.

SECRET #7
OPTION SPREADS TO DEFINE RISK, MARGIN AND MAXIMIZE ROI

When a trader uses a futures contract to trade a market, they are playing a market to simply go up or down. What if you were able to define what you think will happen to a particular market over a specific period of time, and increase your potential profits while defining your risk? This is the idea behind spreading options. Option spreading is the science (and art) of incorporating multiple options to achieve definition in trade design. This chapter will answer the when, why and how to use option spreads.

The benefits to option spreads are numerous. If used properly, option spreading can serve to define risk and reduce and define margin, thereby minimizing cost and maximizing a trade's return on investment (ROI). Option spreads allow definition to trades, which can exploit anticipated market moves while reducing exposure to possible losses.

Option traders face two basic dilemmas when strictly being a buyer or seller of options. Selling options give the trader unlimited risk exposure (which tends to carry high margins) and typically a minimal and defined profit, although probability of success is over-whelmingly on an option seller's side. While exact numbers vary, it is widely known that some 85 to 90 percent of all commodity options expire worthless. This astronomical figure would make even the savviest option buyers think twice about their investment strategy. The majority of option spreads allow a trader to be both a buyer and a seller of options, often creating opportunities to eliminate these two dilemmas of option traders. An option spread can collect premium within the sold option, thus reducing the probability of losing the entire premium of the purchased option (which is used to define the risk of the sold option). Spreading options can often control risk in otherwise uncontrollable environments, and thereby reduce and control margin. This is the key to using option spreads to maximize a trade's ROI (Return On Investment). Let's look at a simple case in point to prove this valuable concept.

For example, with gold at $280/ounce, you purchase a 300 call, and simultaneously sell a 350 call. The 300 call cost you $1,000, while at the same time you collected $300 for selling the 350 call. This bull call spread cost you $700. Assuming you were not intending to make more than five times your investment (defining profit goals), the bull call spread would provide you an opportunity to risk less, have less required margin and achieve a potentially better ROI than simply buying the 300 call. While time value could make this spread less profitable than just buying the 300 call, it typically would result in a better ROI and use up less of your available margin. When you are determining the ROI for this scenario, the long call would be based on an investment of $1,000, while the bull call spread would be based on a $700 investment. Thus, the bull call spread could conceivably return 30% less than the straight long call and still have the same ROI, while requiring less margin and risk exposure. At expiration, if gold is below $300/ounce the straight option would lose $1,000 while the spread would lose $700.

If gold is at $330/ounce at expiration, the straight option would return a profit of $2,000, or 200% (7.1). In turn, the option spread would return a profit of $2,300, or 329% (7.2). Essentially, this spread design benefits similarly from the 300 call as would the straight option, but lessens cost, risk and margin because the trade excepts a predetermined maximum profit (in this case, 50 points or $5,000).

7.1 $3,000 [value of 300 call] - $1,000 [trade cost] = $2,000 profit [200% of $1,000 investment]

7.2 $3,000 [value of 300 call] - $700 [spread cost] - $0 [value of the sold 350 call] = $2,300 profit [329% of $700 investment]

The trick to option spreading is finding the opportunities that exist in markets. Markets act out of the ordinary at times, when volatility, volume or price action shifts from the 'everyday' trade that market participants become accustom. When this occurs, or is expected to occur, option pricing is or will shift and present opportunities that allow a master trader to maximize the combination of risk, reward and probability. A master trader finds opportunities in both normal and abnormal markets by having a keen sense of what market shifts do to option prices and how to take advantage of them.

Volatility is a major element of option pricing, and a simple analysis of how it affects option pricing can make option spreading (and overall trading strategies) more effective and profitable. What follows is a basic if-then analysis table of volatility and market action and their affect on option pricing. Grasping this concept can go a long way to allowing a master trader to identify option strategies quickly, effectively and consistently as seen on the following pages.

IF THE MARKET IS...	AND IS EXPECTED TO...	IF VOLATILITY IS...	AND EXPECTED TO...	THEN YOU SHOULD LOOK TO...
UP	RISE	HIGH	REMAIN HIGH	SHORT BEAR PUT SPREAD OR BEAR PUT RATIO SPREAD
UP	RISE	HIGH	DECLINE	LONG BULL CALL OR RATIO SPREAD
UP	RISE	NEUTRAL	RISE	LONG OTM CALL OR RATIO SPREAD
UP	RISE	NEUTRAL	DECLINE	LONG CALL CALENDAR SPREAD/SHORT PUT BUTTERFLY, CALENDAR OR CONDOR
UP	RISE	LOW	REMAIN LOW	LONG CALL BUTTERFLY OR CONDOR, SHORT PUT BUTTERFLY OR CONDOR
UP	RISE	LOW	RISE	LONG BULL CALL OR RATIO SPREAD
UP	TRADE SIDEWAYS	HIGH	REMAIN HIGH	SHORT STRANGLE, STRADDLE, CONDOR OR BUTTERFLY
UP	TRADE SIDEWAYS	HIGH	DECLINE	SHORT CALL RATIO SPREAD
UP	TRADE SIDEWAYS	NEUTRAL	RISE	SHORT CALL CALENDAR SPREAD
UP	TRADE SIDEWAYS	NEUTRAL	DECLINE	SHORT STRANGLE, STRADDLE, CONDOR, RATIO CALL SPREAD OR BUTTERFLY
UP	TRADE SIDEWAYS	LOW	REMAIN LOW	SHORT ATM CALLS, BUTTERFLY OR CONDOR
UP	TRADE SIDEWAYS	LOW	RISE	LONG ATM (CALL OR PUT) BUTTERFLY OR CONDOR SPREAD

UP	DECLINE	HIGH	REMAIN HIGH	LONG BEAR PUT OR RATIO SPREAD, LONG PUT BUTTERFLY OR CONDOR
UP	DECLINE	HIGH	DECLINE	SHORT SYNTHETIC CALL, BEAR PUT SPREAD, LONG PUT CALENDAR SPREAD
UP	DECLINE	NEUTRAL	RISE	LONG OTM PUTS, BEAR PUT OR RATIO SPREAD, LONG PUT BUTTERFLY OR CONDOR
UP	DECLINE	NEUTRAL	DECLINE	SHORT SYNTHETIC CALL, BEAR PUT SPREAD, LONG PUT CALENDAR SPREAD
UP	DECLINE	LOW	REMAIN LOW	LONG RATIO PUT SPREAD
UP	DECLINE	LOW	RISE	LONG BEAR PUT OR RATIO SPREAD
TRADING SIDEWAYS	TRADE SIDEWAYS	HIGH	REMAIN HIGH	SHORT STRANGLE, STRADDLE OR RATIO SPREAD (CALL OR PUT)
TRADING SIDEWAYS	TRADE SIDEWAYS	HIGH	DECLINE	SHORT STRANGLE, STRADDLE OR RATIO SPREAD (CALL OR PUT)
TRADING SIDEWAYS	TRADE SIDEWAYS	NEUTRAL	RISE	LONG BUTTERFLY OR CONDOR
TRADING SIDEWAYS	TRADE SIDEWAYS	NEUTRAL	DECLINE	SHORT STRANGLE, STRADDLE OR RATIO SPREAD (CALL OR PUT)
TRADING SIDEWAYS	TRADE SIDEWAYS	LOW	REMAIN LOW	LONG BUTTERFLY OR CONDOR

TRADING SIDEWAYS	TRADE SIDEWAYS	LOW	RISE	LONG BUTTERFLY OR CONDOR
DOWN	RISE	HIGH	REMAIN HIGH	LONG BULL CALL OR RATIO SPREAD, LONG CALL BUTTERFLY OR CONDOR
DOWN	RISE	HIGH	DECLINE	SHORT SYNTHETIC PUT, BULL CALL SPREAD, LONG CALL CALENDAR SPREAD
DOWN	RISE	NEUTRAL	RISE	LONG OTM CALLS, BULL CALL OR RATIO SPREAD, LONG CALL BUTTERFLY OR CONDOR
DOWN	RISE	NEUTRAL	DECLINE	SHORT SYNTHETIC PUT, BULL CALL SPREAD, LONG CALL CALENDAR SPREAD
DOWN	RISE	LOW	REMAIN LOW	LONG RATIO CALL SPREAD
DOWN	RISE	LOW	RISE	LONG BULL CALL OR RATIO SPREAD
DOWN	TRADE SIDEWAYS	HIGH	REMAIN HIGH	SHORT STRANGLE, STRADDLE, CONDOR OR BUTTERFLY
DOWN	TRADE SIDEWAYS	HIGH	DECLINE	SHORT PUT RATIO SPREAD
DOWN	TRADE SIDEWAYS	NEUTRAL	RISE	SHORT PUT CALENDAR SPREAD
DOWN	TRADE SIDEWAYS	NEUTRAL	DECLINE	SHORT STRANGLE, STRADDLE, CONDOR, RATIO CALL SPREAD OR BUTTERFLY
DOWN	TRADE SIDEWAYS	LOW	REMAIN LOW	SHORT ATM PUTS, BUTTERFLY OR CONDOR

DOWN	TRADE SIDEWAYS	LOW	RISE	LONG ATM (CALL OR PUT) BUTTERFLY OR CONDOR SPREAD
DOWN	DECLINE	HIGH	REMAIN HIGH	LONG BULL CALL SPREADS OR BULL CALL RATIO SPREADS
DOWN	DECLINE	HIGH	DECLINE	LONG BEAR PUT OR RATIO SPREAD
DOWN	DECLINE	NEUTRAL	RISE	LONG OTM PUTS OR RATIO SPREAD
DOWN	DECLINE	NEUTRAL	DECLINE	LONG PUT CALENDAR SPREAD/SHORT CALL BUTTERFLY, CALENDAR OR CONDOR
DOWN	DECLINE	LOW	REMAIN LOW	LONG PUT BUTTERFLY OR CONDOR, SHORT CALL BUTTERFLY OR CONDOR
DOWN	DECLINE	LOW	RISE	LONG BEAR PUT RATIO SPREAD

Knowing when, why and how to apply option spreads to your overall trading strategy is vital to adding this important tool to your arsenal of trade tactics. Along with applying your understanding of volatility as it affects option prices, the following breakdown will provide you with a grasp of many common option spreads and their proper application.

Spread	When to use it	Why to use it	How to use it
Bear Call	The market is expected to maintain current price level or go down	Allows for the selling of option premium, but has defined risk and margin	Sell an ATM or NTM call and buy an OTM call (1-to1)
Bear Put	The market is expected to go down, but downside is predefined	Provides ATM or NTM put price action at a reduced cost & risk	Buy an ATM or NTM put and sell an OTM put (1-to-1)
Bull Call	The market is expected to go up, but upside is predefined	Provides ATM or NTM call price action at a reduced cost & risk	Buy an ATM or NTM call and sell an OTM call (1-to-1)
Bull Put	The market is expected to maintain current price level or go up	Allows for the selling of option premium, but has defined risk and margin	Sell an ATM or NTM put and buy an OTM put (1-to-1)
Butterfly (Long Call)	The market is expected to rise slightly or slowly trend upwards	Makes a bull call spread less expensive but profits less on a move beyond the short side of the trade	Buy 1 NTM, sell 2 OTM and buy 1 further OTM (1 to (2) to 1, spread by equidistant strike prices)

Strategy	Market Outlook	Characteristics	Construction
Butterfly (Long Put)	The market is expected to stay flat or move slightly to the downside	Makes a bear put spread less expensive but profits less on a move beyond the short side of the trade	Buy 1 NTM, sell 2 OTM and buy 1 further OTM (1 to (2) to 1, spread by equidistant strike prices)
Butterfly (Short Call)	The market is expected to stay flat or move slightly to the downside	Low margin, low risk way of betting against an up market	Sell 1 ATM, buy 2 OTM and sell 1 further OTM ((1) to 2 to (1), spread by equidistant strike prices)
Butterfly (Short Put)	The market is expected to stay flat or move slightly to the upside	Low margin, low risk way of betting against a down market	Sell 1 ATM, buy 2 OTM and sell 1 further OTM ((1) to 2 to (1), spread by equidistant strike prices)
Calendar (Call) Long near term Short long term	The market is expected to trend or spike upwards in the short term	Low margin, low risk way of a playing a short term break in the market	Buy a near term futures month call, and sell a long term futures month call farther OTM
Calendar (Call) Short near term Long long term	The market is expected to trend or rise long term, and maintain prices or go down short term	Reduces cost of a long term play; maximizes time value depreciation of near term option	Sell a near term futures month call OTM, and buy a long term futures month call closer OTM

Calendar (Put) Short near term Long long term	The market is expected to trend or decline long term, and maintain prices or go up short term	Reduces cost of a long term play; maximizes time value depreciation of near term option	Sell a near term futures month put OTM, and buy a long term futures month put closer OTM
Calendar (Put) Long near term Short long term	The market is expected to trend or spike downwards in the short term	Low margin, low risk way of playing a short term break in the market	Buy a near term futures month put, and sell a long term futures month put farther OTM
Condor (Long Call)	The market is expected to stay flat or move slightly to the upside	Low margin, low risk way of playing a small move to the upside	Buy 1 NTM, sell 1 OTM, sell 1 further OTM and buy 1 even further OTM (use strike price spacing for trade definition)
Condor (Long Put)	The market is expected to stay flat or move slightly to the downside	Low margin, low risk way of playing a small move to the downside	Buy 1 NTM, sell 1 OTM, sell 1 further OTM and buy 1 even further OTM (use strike price spacing for trade definition)

Condor (Short Call)	The market is expected to go down or completely breakout to the upside	Low margin, low risk way of shorting a NTM call or playing a breakout to the upside	Sell 1 NTM, buy 1 OTM, buy 1 further OTM and sell 1 even further OTM (use strike price spacing for trade definition)
Condor (Short Put)	The market is expected to go up or completely breakout to the downside	Low margin, low risk way of shorting a NTM put or playing a breakout to the downside	Sell 1 NTM, buy 1 OTM, buy 1 further OTM and sell 1 even further OTM (use strike price spacing for trade definition)
Ratio Call (Long)	The market is expected to completely breakout to the upside	Allows for the selling of option premium, but has unlimited upside potential on a large price move	Sell 1 NTM, buy 2 (or more) OTM; using 3,4 or 5 increases cost and potential gains on a rally
Ratio Call (Short)	The market is expected to go up slightly, stay flat or go down; but not to breakout to the upside	Offsets cost of long NTM call but has unlimited risk on a large upside rally	Buy 1 NTM, sell 2 (or more) OTM; using 3,4 or 5 decreases cost but increases risk exposure

Ratio Put (Long)	The market is expected to completely breakout to the downside	Allows for the selling of option premium, but has unlimited upside potential on a large price move	Sell 1 NTM, buy 2 (or more) OTM; using 3,4 or 5 increases cost and potential gains on a rally
Ratio Put (Short)	The market is expected to go down slightly, stay flat or go up; but not to breakout to the downside	Offsets cost of long NTM call but has unlimited risk on a large selloff	Buy 1 NTM, sell 2 (or more) OTM; using 3,4 or 5 decreases cost but increases risk exposure
Straddle (Long)	Volatility is expected to rise, and price action is expected to increase, but direction is unknown	Allows for the playing of a market's volatility rise rather than knowing the direction	Buy 1 ATM call, buy 1 ATM put
Straddle (Short)	Volatility is expected to go down & price action should decrease while the market is expected to stay flat	Maximizes the collection of option premium in a flat market with dying volatility	Sell 1 ATM call, sell 1 ATM put

Strategy	Market Outlook	Purpose	Construction
Strangle (Long)	Volatility is expected to rise, and price action is expected to increase, but direction is unknown	Allows for the playing of a market's volatility rise rather than knowing the direction	Buy 1 NTM call, buy 1 NTM put (going further OTM reduces cost but needs a larger price move
Strangle (Short)	Volatility is expected to go down & price action should decrease while the market is expected to stay flat	Maximizes the collection of option premium in a flat market with dying volatility	Sell 1 NTM call, sell 1 NTM put (going further OTM decreases risk but reduces profit as well

A master trader is always seeking out opportunities, analyzing the market for changes and fluctuations, furthering their education and grasp of market knowledge. A master trader knows the 'home run' and 'can't miss' trades are not the way to making a consistent profit trading commodities. An overall comprehension and both a macro and micro outlook of markets are how successful traders consistently profit from trading in futures and options. "7 Secrets" has shown you the path to having the knowledge and application skills necessary to become a master trader. It is up to you to take this base and grow to the ranks of a master.

Market Art!

Market-related art available through

Traders Press, Inc.®

The print pictured on the front cover of this book, as well as a varied selection of other market-related artwork and gifts are available exclusively through *Traders Press, Inc.®*
Currently available items are pictured on our wesite at *http://www.traderspress.com* and in our Traders Catalog, which is available
FREE upon request

or contact us at:
800-927-8222 ~ 864-298-0222
Fax 864-298-0221

Traders Press, Inc.®
PO Box 6206
Greenville, SC 29606

Serving Traders since 1975

TRADERS PRESS, INC.®
PO BOX 6206
GREENVILLE, SC 29606

7 Secrets Every Commodity Trader Needs to Know (Mound)
A Complete Guide to Trading Profits (Paris)
A Professional Look at S&P Day Trading (Trivette)
A Treasury of Wall Street Wisdom (Editors: Schultz & Coslow)
Ask Mr. EasyLanguage (Tennis)
Beginner's Guide to Computer Assisted Trading (Alexander)
Channels and Cycles: A Tribute to J.M. Hurst (Millard)
Chart Reading for Professional Traders (Jenkins)
Commodity Spreads: Analysis, Selection and Trading Techniques (Smith)
Comparison of Twelve Technical Trading Systems (Lukac, Brorsen, & Irwin)
Complete Stock Market Trading and Forecasting Course (Jenkins)
Cyclic Analysis (J.M. Hurst)
Dynamic Trading (Miner)
Exceptional Trading: The Mind Game (Roosevelt)
Fibonacci Ratios with Pattern Recognition (Pesavento)
Futures Spread Trading: The Complete Guide (Smith)
Geometry of Markets (Gilmore)
Geometry of Stock Market Profits (Jenkins)
Harmonic Vibrations (Pesavento)
How to Trade in Stocks (Livermore & Smitten)
Hurst Cycles Course (J.M. Hurst)
Investing by the Stars (Weingarten)
It's Your Option (Zelkin)
Magic of Moving Averages (Lowry)
Market Rap: The Odyssey of a Still-Struggling Commodity Trader (Collins)
Pit Trading: Do You Have the Right Stuff? (Hoffman)
Planetary Harmonics of Speculative Markets (Pesavento)
Point & Figure Charting (Aby)
Point & Figure Charting: Commodity and Stock Trading Techniques (Zieg)
Private Thoughts From a Trader's Diary (Pesavento & MacKay)
Profitable Grain Trading (Ainsworth)
Profitable Patterns for Stock Trading (Pesavento)
RoadMap to the Markets (Busby)
Short-Term Trading with Price Patterns (Harris)
Single Stock Futures: The Complete Guide (Greenberg)
Stock Patterns for Day Trading (2 volumes) (Rudd)
Stock Trading Based on Price Patterns (Harris)
Study Helps in Point & Figure Techniques (Wheelan)
Technically Speaking (Wilkinson)
Technical Trading Systems for Commodities and Stocks (Patel)
The Amazing Life of Jesse Livermore: World's Greatest Stock Trader (Smitten)
The Handbook of: Global Securities Operations (O'Connell & Steiniger)
The Opening Price Principle: The Best Kept Secret on Wall Street (Pesavento & MacKay)
The Professional Commodity Trader (Kroll)
The Taylor Trading Technique (Taylor)
The Trading Rule That Can Make You Rich* (Dobson)
Top Traders Under Fire (Collins)
Trading Secrets of the Inner Circle (Goodwin)
Trading S&P Futures and Options (Lloyd)
Twelve Habitudes of Highly Successful Traders (Roosevelt)
Understanding Bollinger Bands (Dobson)
Understanding Fibonacci Numbers (Dobson)
Viewpoints of a Commodity Trader (Longstreet)
Wall Street Ventures & Adventures Through Forty Years (Wyckoff)
Winning Edge 4 (Toghraie)
Winning Market Systems (Appel)

**Please contact Traders Press to receive our current catalog describing these and
many other books and gifts of interest to investors and traders.
800-927-8222 ~ 864-298-0222 ~ fax 864-298-0221 ~ traderspress.com ~
customerservice@traderspress.com**